Productivity, Efficiency and Pricing in India Post

About the Author

Dr. S.K. Sinha is a Ph D in Economics from Mumbai University. He started his career as Lecturer in Economics in Hansraj College, Delhi University. In 1979 he joined the Indian Postal Service (Department of Posts, Government of India). In his career of 30 years he has served India Post in Maharashtra, Western Uttar Pradesh, Bihar, West Bengal, and difficult hilly and tribal states of Sikkim, and North-East. Presently, a very senior officer of India Post, he has worked in various capacities at state headquarters and as regional head entrusted with the management of human resources and materials, directed towards optimizing postal operation at all levels. Besides, being closely and actively involved in implementing technology at the grassroot level in post offices, he was also associated with the planning and policy formulations at the state level, and also headed the Corporate Planning Division of India Post for almost two years.

Productivity, Efficiency and Pricing in India Post

Shekhar Kumar Sinha

CONCEPT PUBLISHING COMPANY, NEW DELHI-110059

ISBN 13: 978-81-8069-649-7 **ISBN 10: 81-8069-649-9**

First Published 2009

Published and Printed by

Concept
Since 1974

Concept Publishing Company

Regd. Office:

A/15-16, Commercial Block, Mohan Garden
New Delhi-110059 (India)
Phones: 25351460, 25351794, *Fax*: 091-11-25357109
Email: publishing@conceptpub.com,
Website: www.conceptpub.com

Editorial Office:

H-13, Bali Nagar, New Delhi-110 015, India.

Cataloging in Publication Data--*Courtesy:* D.K. Agencies (P) Ltd. <docinfo@dkagencies.com>

Sinha, Shekhar Kumar.
Productivity, efficiency and pricing in India Post / Shekhar Kumar Sinha.
p. cm.
Originally presented as the author's thesis (Ph. D.)--University of Mumbai.
Includes bibliographical references (p.).
Includes index.
ISBN 13: 9788180696497 ISBN 10: 8180696499

1. India. Post Office. 2. Postal rates--India. 3. Postal service--Government policy--India. I. Title.

DDC 383.230954 22

Dedicated to

My Parents and My Elder Brother

Who are No More

Preface

The experience of rapid economic development in many developing countries, especially those in East Asia, has been engaging the attention of development economists in particular. Productivity and efficiency as source of growth is the simplest of all ideas. Over the last quarter of century issues of productivity and efficiency has become more central (and also more contentious) in public debates and arguments, and has, therefore, been the subject of much research.

For postal administrations, the reasons for study of productivity and efficiency are even more pressing. Of late, administrations in may industrialized countries and elsewhere are facing a diminished portion, or an abolition of reserved areas and/or increasing competition from new entrants such as private delivery companies in liberalized framework of postal markets. For these postal administrations to fulfill the Universal Service Obligations, there is a need to focus on increasing operational efficiency and productivity, so as to enable them to preserve a fair and affordable postal rate. This applies with equal, if not more, urgency to India Post which, with more than 1,38,000 post offices in rural areas touches the lives of people more intimately than, perhaps, another government agency. In fact the importance of improved efficiency and productivity was never felt as critical in the last three decades as it is today for survival and sustained viability of postal services in India.

Monumental literature on productivity and efficiency has developed and dramatically expanded since the early 1970s. Review of the relevant literature showed that considerable work has been done on estimating productivity and efficiency of postal administrations of advanced industrial countries of Europe, USA, Australia, and Japan, but no such attempts have been undertaken in the context of developing economies like India. Significantly, substantial progress has been made towards understanding productivity and efficiency characteristics of industries, services sector like banks and railways in India, but in contrast similar studies in the postal sector are woefully lacking.

An effort has, therefore, been made towards filling an important gap in the literature on productivity and efficiency of postal sector in India. Productivity and efficiency of resources used in India Post have been examined to see how they have changed over a period of time. The work was motivated by the general approach of looking for lessons for India Post, with primary focus of attention on the direct role of productivity and efficiency in enhancing social opportunities. The study also draws on comparison of India Post's performance with those of other countries, Asian and global, and emerging economies. Besides the findings that productivity of India Post is either stagnating or declining, surplus manpower and capital resources are also observed. Guidelines for policy framework have been indicated to ensure balance between efficiency and equity, as also several measures to face increased competition in the liberalized/ globalize market.

It is hoped that the work would generate further studies and research on the postal sector. For those interested in pursuing a study on the postal sector, or in order to help students who are embarking on a course of serious study on postal sector, I have tired to provide reasonably comprehensive references to the formal literature which has grown and flourished, on productivity, efficiency, and pricing of postal sector. I am quite conscious of the inadequacy of the bibliography as a guide to serious students.

Acknowledgements

This book is based primarily on the doctoral thesis submitted to the University of Mumbai. I would, therefore, like to express my sincere and deep gratitude to Prof. S. Sriraman, Walchand Hirachand, Professor of Transport Economics, Department of Economics, University of Mumbai who guided me on the subject. Without his support I could not possibly have completed this study.

I would also like to put on record my sincere gratitude to my senior school and college colleague, Professor Raghvendra Jha for giving valuable insights during the exploratory phase of my study. I would also like to thank Professor (Retd.) K.L. Krishna of the Delhi School of Economics for his valuable suggestions. I am particularly grateful to all my colleagues who studied with me at the Delhi School of Economics especially those who are presently holding very high positions in the academic field, as for example Prof. Ashima Goel of Indira Gandhi Institute of Developmental Research, Mumbai. I am also grateful to Professor S. Perelman of the University of Liege for providing me some of his papers on postal studies which I found extremely difficult to obtain. His immediate response to any clarification which I sought from him relating to my work through e-mail also greatly facilitated my work.

I would also like to put on record my sincere thanks to the librarian and staff of the Indira Gandhi Institute of Development Research, Mumbai and the Ratan Tata Library, Delhi School of Economics. Special mention needs to be made of Shri Manjunath, Librarian, Indira Gandhi Institute of Development Research, Mumbai who went out of his way to help me in providing me with various articles and books. I would also like to thank the staff of the Jawaharlal Nehru Library, University of Mumbai for the cooperation extended to me.

I would like to thank the Professors of the Department of Economics, University of Mumbai who were helpful to me throughout the course of my study. I am also grateful to the administrative staff of the Department of Economics particularly, Mrs. Pawar (who was earlier in the Department) and Mr. Ajit Patil for the help extended to me.

Last, but not the least, I am specially grateful to my fellow research colleagues such as Dr. Anand Venkatesh, Jerome Monteiro, Vidya Mohite, Mahendra Parihar and Nitin Ghag who not only provided me with very valuable suggestions and inputs but also assisted me in a substantial manner during the course of my work, more so towards the end. I would also like to put on record my gratitude to all the officers and staff of the Department of Posts, specially Shri Vivek Dhavne, Postal Assistant for helping me in collecting the requisite data.

Contents

LIST OF TABLES AND FIGURES

List of Tables

List of Figures

List of Abbreviations

ABC	Activity Based Costing
ACM	Attributed Cost Method
AE	Allocative Efficiency
BE	Budget Estimates
CB	Central Budget
COLS	Corrected Ordinary Least Squares
COUS	Cost of Universal Service
CPG	China Post Group
CPI	Consumer Price Index
CRS	Constant Returns to Scale
DA	Dearness Allowance
DAP	Delivery-Area Access Pricing
DAVP	Directorate of Audio Visual Publicity
DEA	Data Envelopment Analysis
DEAP	Data Envelopment Analysis Programme
DG	Director General
DMU	Decision Making Unit
DoP	Department of Posts
ECT	Empresa Brasileira de Correios e Telegrafos
EP	Entry Pricing
FDC	Fully Distributed Cost
FDH	Free Disposal Hull
GoI	Government of India
GP	Gram Panchayat
GPO	General Post Office
HPO	Head Post Office
IPD	Indian Postal Department
IPOs	Initial Public Offers
IPS	Indian Postal System
IRF	Input Requirement Frontier
IRS	Increasing Returns to Scale

LP	Linear Programming
LR	Likelihood Ratio
ML	Maximum Likelihood
MoF	Ministry of Finance
MPI	Malmquist Productivity Index
MSC	Management Sectional Centre
NABARD	National Bank for Agriculture and Rural Development
NAC	Net Avoided Cost Method
NIRS	Non-Increasing Returns to Scale
NREGS	National Rural Employment Guarantee Scheme
OLS	Ordinary Least Squares
P&T	Posts and Telegraph
P.C	Price Cap
PCI	Postal Circles in India
PCR	Price-cap Regulation
PLI	Postal Life Insurance
PO	Post Office
PPO	Public Postal Operators
PSB	Postal Services Board
RMS	Railway Mail Service
ROM	Ratio of Output Method
ROR	Rate of Return Regulation
RPLI	Rural Postal Life Insurance
RRM	Ratio of Revenue Method
SBI	State Bank of India
SE	Scale Efficiency
SFA	Stochastic Frontier Analysis
SFM	Stochastic Frontier Method
TE	Technical Efficiency
TFP	Total Factor Productivity
UPU	Universal Postal Union
USO	Universal Service Obligations
VRS	Variable Returns to Scale

1

Introduction

1.1 Background

Productivity and Efficiency in the use of scarce resources are of immense concern in a developing economy like India. As a source of growth, productivity has moved to the centre stage in the analysis of growth of developing countries in recent years. It is recognized today as a key feature of economic dynamism. Earlier, many considered productivity growth and technical progress as synonymous but now there is a widely accepted view that there is a distinction between the two.

Productivity change was initially attributed exclusively to shifts in the production technology (the magnitude of actual technical change). Eventually, roles were also assigned to biases of technical change and the structure of technology (scale economies). Moreover, the presumption that firms/organisations would realize maximum potential output, given the input, or alternatively, would use minimum input given the output was not necessarily applicable in reality. This brought in the concept of efficiency. Productivity would vary not only due to differences in production technology but also due to differences in the efficiency with which inputs are converted into outputs. Efficiency change, therefore, provides an independent contribution to productivity. In fact, if efficiency change is omitted from the analysis, there would be an overestimation of unexplained residuals which Abramovitz (1956) appropriately referred to as a measure of ignorance about the causes of economic growth, and also to an erroneous allocation of productivity change to its included sources.

There has been an increasing interest in measuring productivity and, more specially, efficiency. This is because measurement of productivity and efficiency enables one to quantify differentials that are predicted qualitatively by theory. For example, there is a common belief that productive efficiency is a survival condition in a competitive environment and that its importance diminishes as competitive pressure subsides. Such a belief or otherwise can be established only by studies on productivity and efficiency measurement. Similarly, the effects of regulation, ownership (public or private), etc. on productivity and efficiency differentials can be assessed only by such studies.

Moreover, a study of productivity measures enables an evaluation of production units. Only by measuring productivity and efficiency and separating their effects from the effects of production environment, one can possibly explore hypotheses concerning the sources of productivity or efficiency differentials. Such an identification of sources is essential for the initiation of public policies designed to improve the performance of production units. The quantification of productivity and efficiency would also provide managements with a control mechanism with which to monitor the performance of units under their control. This may be quite important from a policy perspective since, for example, a slow down in productivity growth due to increased inefficiency may suggest different policies to be undertaken as compared to a situation such as a slowdown due to a lack of technical change. For example, slow productivity growth due to inefficiency may be due to institutional barriers to diffusion of innovations. In this case, policies to remove these barriers may be more effective in improving productivity than policies directed at innovation. Economics, management science and public administration literature contain numerous examples of the use of efficiency/ productivity measurement for this purpose.

For postal administrations, the reasons for a study of productivity and efficiency may be even more pressing. Traditionally, postal administrations all over the world have been under a Universal Service Obligation (USO) clause to provide a minimum defined service(s) to all persons at uniform and affordable rates. The loss on account of performing these services have all along been made up elsewhere because of the monopoly position of postal administrations. Of late, these administrations in many industrialized countries and elsewhere are facing a diminished portion or an abolition of the reserved areas and/or increasing competition from new entrants such as private delivery companies in a liberalized framework of postal markets. This situation is also being faced by India Post which is the corporate name adopted by the Indian Postal System run by the Government of India. For postal administrations like India Post to fulfil their Universal Service Obligations, they need to focus more on increasing operational efficiency and productivity so as to enable them to preserve a fair and affordable postal rate.

Moreover, for public utilities like the postal system, the market is an ineffective way of taking care of the productivity and efficiency of a decision-making unit through the pricing mechanism. The pricing policy which is followed such as a policy of Price-Cap Regulation (PCR) or the Rate of Return Regulation (ROR) has a significant impact on productivity and efficiency. PCR, in which the so-called X factor is also used for a pricing cap, places excessive reliance on productivity measures. The X factor is sometimes called "the productivity offset". If set sufficiently high, it would put the firm under pressure to be efficient. Under ROR, while regulating the fixation of prices, the firm is allowed revenues sufficient to cover its operating expenses plus a return on assets that are employed in service to the public. If the permitted rate of return exceeds the cost of capital, the public utility may want to use more assets than is efficient. Also, as the firm's own costs are used to determine its revenues, an inefficient firm may simply be allowed higher prices and more revenues to cover its higher costs. Needless to say, the incentive for efficiency or innovation is weakened in such circumstances. Thus, a study on productivity and efficiency, where some kind of regulation is inherent by the very nature of the product/service such as those in the case of post offices, would not be complete without looking into the pricing aspect of postal services.

1.2 India Post—An Overview

Given below is a brief overview of India Post in terms of its evolution, its organizational structure, its operational schemes and some of the recent developments which have had an impact on its present status as a significant player in the context of postal services in India.

1.2.1 Evolution of India Post

The history of Indian Post Office dates back to 1688 when the first Post Office was established at Mumbai by the East India Company. It was made available for private communications on payment of postage in 1774. In 1837, the Indian Post Office Act was promulgated which abolished private posts and gave monopoly to official post offices for carrying letters. An All India Postal system integrating the Postal Services of the three Presidencies was established. In 1854, the Imperial Post Office Act was promulgated under which the entire Department with 652 post offices and four Postmasters General were placed under a Central Organization headed by a Director General. In 1898, the Indian Post Office Act was enacted which provided a legislative basis to the Department of Posts for its various services.

Prior to independence, the Postal Service was being run on profit and was a source of revenue for the Government. Thereafter, opening of post offices was being subsidized to the extent of Rs. 750 per annum. Presently, the subsidy given to post offices in rural areas ranges from 66.67 per cent in normal areas to 85 per cent in hilly, tribal and desert areas. This policy of giving a subsidy was justified on the ground that the Department is under a Universal Service Obligation (USO) to provide postal services within the reach of every person in the country at a uniform/affordable price. However, it has had a cascading effect on the deficit of the Department which was Rs. 1511.44 crore in 2007-08.

Prior to 1985, there was no separate budget for the Department of Posts and the losses of the Department on account of postal services were covered by the Telecom services as the then P&T Department was always showing a net surplus in its revenue expenditure statement. Subsequent to the bifurcation of the then P&T Department into the Department of Posts and the Department of Telecommunications, postal services incurred a net revenue deficit of Rs. 163.55 crores, Rs. 216.43 crore and Rs. 190.87 crore during the period 1985-86, 1986-87 and 1987-88 respectively. This deficit has been showing an increasing trend and was Rs. 1511.44 crore in 2007-08. Financial self-sufficiency is, therefore, an important issue for the Department of Posts. Indeed, self-sufficiency has been one of the objectives in the 9th, 10th and 11th Five Year Plans.

1.2.2 *Organisational Structure of India Post*

The Department of Posts (i.e. India Post) forms a part of the Ministry of Communications and Information Technology, Government of India and is headed by the Minister of Communications and Information Technology. It is responsible for the planning, development, expansion, operation and maintenance of postal services in the country. It also discharges certain agency functions in respect of savings bank and other small savings schemes, life insurance, and disbursements of pensions, etc.

The Postal Services Board is the apex management body of the Department comprising the Chairman (who is also the Secretary, Department of Posts and Director General, Posts) and six Members. For providing postal services, the whole country has been divided into 22 Postal circles. Each circle is co-terminus with a State except the North Eastern circle which comprises six North Eastern States, the Maharashtra circle which includes Goa, the West Bengal circle which includes Sikkim and the Union Territory of Andaman and Nicobar Islands, the Kerala circle which includes the Union Territory of Lakshadweep and the Punjab circle which includes the Union Territory of Chandigarh. A Chief Postmaster General heads each circle. Each circle is divided into regions comprising groups of field units called divisions (Postal/Railway Mail Service divisions). Each region is headed by a Postmaster General who is a very Senior Manager of the area. The regions are further divided into divisions which are headed by the Senior Superintendent or the Superintendent. In the circles and regions, there are other functional supporting logistical units like Stamp Depots, Stores Depots and Mail Motor Service.

Post Offices in the country are categorized as Head, Sub and Branch Post Offices. Gramin Dak Sewa Post Offices are located in rural areas and are run by the Gramin Dak Sewaks who are not regular departmental employees, but function as agents of the Department. The sub-post offices are departmental offices located in both rural and urban areas, and are manned by departmental employees. The head post offices are graded into five categories according to their workload and staff strength, the largest being the General Post Office (GPO) at the circle headquarters.

The number of post offices in India increased from 22,116 in 1947 to 1,55,204 in March 2007. This rapid growth in the number of post offices is the result of a conscious decision at the start of planned development to spread the postal network widely in accordance with the social responsibility feature of the postal sector. Consequently, a large number of post offices were planned to be opened in each of the Five Year Plans—19000 in the 1st Five Year Plan, 22000 in the 2nd Five Year Plan, 17000 in the 3rd Five Year Plan and 31000 in the 4th Five Year Plan and so on. As a result of this massive expansion of Postal network, the Indian postal network is the largest in the world. The number of post offices is much higher than in a country like China which has a greater population and larger area than India. One post office in India serves 7160 persons covering an area of approximately 22.2. sq. kms and compares very favourably with China (one post office serves 19962 people and covers 145 sq. kms). Despite this network, out of 5.95 lakh inhabited villages, less than one-third villages are having post offices. Moreover, against 2.34 lakh Gram Panchayat villages, only 1.15 lakh Gram Panchayat villages have post offices.

1.2.3 Schemes of India Post

India Post handles a large number of products such as all types of mails, parcels, and money remittances. It also provides value added services such as registration, insurance, express services, besides doing agency and retail functions.

The Post Office Savings Bank scheme is the single largest source of revenue for the Department with a customer base of 17.2 crore account holders with a total amount deposited of Rs. 3.5 lakh crore as on 31-03-2007. A branch network double the size of all the banks in the country put together and with a diverse product range, the Post Office Savings Bank is the largest retail banking network in the country. This Post Office Savings Bank functions as an agency of the Ministry of Finance, Government of India. The Ministry of Finance pays an annual remuneration to the Department of Posts for the performance of the savings bank function. The Department has also taken several initiatives for disbursal of social security schemes such as old age pension scheme, NREGS, etc. through the rural postal network. So far more than 2.0 crore savings bank accounts have been opened for disbursal of wages to the NREGS beneficiaries.

Some of the other major initiatives which have been undertaken by the Department include disbursal of micro credit to women Self

Help Groups as a pilot project in collaboration with NABARD (National Bank for Agriculture and Rural Development). The Department has also tied-up with the State Bank of India on a pilot basis for sourcing their assets, liability and investment products through the vast network of India Post. An agreement has also been signed between the Department and State Bank of India in this connection. Smart Card accounts are being operated through a point of sale device which consists of a mobile phone instrument, biometric card to check the identification of the account holders and a battery operated printer. The day-to-day transactions are updated immediately with the back end server which is centrally located at the State Bank of India office in Mumbai.

The Postal Life Insurance (PLI) is another product of the Department which is in operation since 1884. Initially designed for postal employees, today it caters to employees of not only of the Central and State Governments but also of local bodies, Government aided educational institutions, universities, public sector undertakings, banks, etc. As a major initiative towards fulfilling social commitment, the Rural Postal Life Insurance (RPLI) scheme was introduced in 1995 for insuring the lives of the people living in rural areas. The PLI/RPLI corpus is Rs. 15,960 crore. The Department proposes to convert this into tradable securities over a period of 3 years.

1.2.4 Recent Developments

The existing Postal system, as it has emerged over a period of time, has led to a situation where private couriers are cream-skimming the profitable sector of the market, i.e. the urban and the metro sectors, leaving the unprofitable areas, i.e. the vast rural areas to the Department of Posts for performing the postal services. Neither is there any regulatory authority nor is there any contribution from these private couriers towards fulfilling the USO. It has been the position of the Department of Posts that a major chunk of the deficit of the Department, which was Rs. 1511.44 crores in 2007-08, is on account of fulfilling the USO.

Despite having legal provisions in place to protect them from competition, post offices are actually facing competition in all the markets. Traditional mail items are under threat from electronic substitution that is spreading and for every post office service, there is alternative supplier in most cases. In the express segment dealing with parcels and packages, there are competitors who are local couriers or multi-nationals like DHL, UPS, Fedex, etc. In the financial segment dealing with the savings, money orders, the competitors are the banks and established multi-national companies such as Western Union, Money Gram. The local shops, kiosks are threat to the retailing activities of the post offices. In the logistics segment relating to warehousing, packaging, distribution, the transportation companies are the competitors.

To effectively meet this competition, post offices all over the world are trying to become more commercially focused and are starting to diversify into new services. This is being done with increasing partnership with private sector companies that value the reach of postal networks. Post offices are also attempting to change their traditional institutional setup. They are moving away from the typical public administration model and moving towards private status with an international presence. For example, Deutsche Post is no longer a German post office but a worldwide leader in logistics. To counter growing competition, post offices must be given more commercial freedom through, increased autonomy from Government control, which has been the experience in the European Union. Independent regulation may be introduced to protect customer interest and ensure a level playing field.

With more than 1,38,000 Post Offices in rural areas, India Post touches the lives of people more intimately than, perhaps, another Government agency. It has traditionally been found to be an indispensable tool of mass communication and for rapid dissemination of information amongst people. It has continued to be an important aid to the development of industry, trade, and commerce and has immense scope in facilitating e-commerce. The importance of improved efficiency and productivity was never felt as critical in the last three decades as it is today for survival and sustained viability of postal service in India. With advanced statistical methodologies and measurement techniques, substantial progress has been made towards understanding productivity, efficiency characteristic of banks and industries in the developed countries. In contrast, similar studies in the service sector especially the postal sector have never been seriously attempted in developing countries, more so in India though some preliminary work on productivity was undertaken by the Expert Committee on Excellence in Postal Service (Government of India, 1988) which examined the productivity of the Indian Postal Department in the late eighties covering the period during 1950s to mid-1980s.

1.3 Statement of the Problem

Given the background of a growing concern over productivity, efficiency and also increasing deficits of India Post, this study is a critical evaluation of productivity, efficiency and also pricing of India Post. Appropriate policies that can be adopted in regard to these aspects, taking into consideration emerging market conditions, is also discussed.

1.4 Objectives of the Study

- (i) To examine whether resources are being utilized in the most productive and efficient manner.
- (ii) To critically examine the existing price mechanism being followed in India Post and how it relates to cost recovery.
- (iii) To identify pricing principles for cost recovery from the optimal pricing literature.
- (iv) To derive a pricing scheme consistent with cost minimization and various objectives of the Department.
- (v) To formulate guidelines for policy framework which can ensure maximum productivity and efficiency of resources and optimal pricing procedures.

1.5 Methodological Approach to the Study

The study looks at the productivity and efficiency of the resources used in India Post and sees how they have changed over a period of time. This would help in formulating guidelines for ensuring maximum productivity and efficiency in resource-utilization. Pricing schemes aimed at recovery of costs of the products/services is examined from the point of view of feasibility and applicability in consonance with the objectives of the Postal Department. Further, given the tendency for existing price policies to undermine cost reductions, an appropriate policy framework that seeks to promote measures aimed at increasing revenue and minimizing cost is discussed, which can ensure that price policy reforms are well designed to take care of relevant and appropriate cost recovery.

1.6 Chapter Scheme of the Study

The study has been divided into seven Chapters including the introductory Chapter.

Chapter 2 begins with an overview on productivity and efficiency in terms of the general insights offered to us in the literature on productivity and efficiency since 1950s. This is followed by a critical look at the literature from the point of view of particular sector insights mainly relating to public utilities like railways, electric companies, insurance companies and post offices. Thereafter, a review of pricing and costing literature especially in the context of postal services is taken up. In the last section of this Chapter, the issues that emerged from the reviews on productivity, efficiency and pricing of postal sector are taken up for detailed analysis in the study.

The detailed methodology of the study is outlined in Chapter 3. After describing the broad approach that has been adopted for the study, the non-parametric method followed for estimating the productivity and efficiency of India Post is specified. This is followed by a discussion of the parametric method for estimating technical efficiency. Also spelt out is the approach to an analysis to pricing of postal services with a view to develop an appropriate costing methodology. Issues relating to data are also discussed in this chapter.

Chapter 4 provides the empirical results on productivity and efficiency of India Post along with a detailed analysis of these results that attempts a comparison of the position of India Post on a global basis in the context of the developing economies. Further, an attempt has also been made to make a comparison of India Post with the developing economies of Asia and then with reference to the group of emerging economies, the E-7 (China, India, Brazil, Russia, Indonesia, Mexico, and Turkey). The last part reflects the results of the empirical estimation on the productivity and efficiency of postal circles of India Post.

Chapter 5 discusses pricing issues in fairly great detail in the context of India Post. After providing a comprehensive description of the current costing methodology followed by India Post, some new approaches have been outlined that can be undertaken in respect of costing and pricing in India Post. This outline includes a proposal relating to work sharing and access pricing which may be taken up for consideration by India Post as part of its pricing regime in the context of an emerging liberalized market structure for postal services. In Chapter 6, the various policy implications that emerge from the study are examined. This discussion forms the basis for policy guidelines for India Post.

Finally, Chapter 7 provides a summary of the study, the main findings and the concluding remarks.

2

Insights from the Literature

2.1 Productivity and Efficiency: An Overview

Productivity is represented by the ratio of total product (output) to the amount of input used during the same period. The earliest approach to measurement of productivity was based upon a ratio of index of aggregate output to a single input, typically, labour. The productivity ratio was normalized to some base year thereby giving an index of productivity overtime. Though having the advantage of computational simplicity, it was difficult to identify the causal factors accounting for increased growth such as use of more capital, realization of economies of scale, etc. This led to measuring productivity using a ratio of index of aggregate output to an index of aggregate inputs. This was the concept of Total Factor Productivity (TFP).

One approach to measuring productivity involved the explicit specification of a production function and direct linkage of productivity growth to the key characteristics or parameters of the function. The pioneering paper in developing this approach is that of Solow (1957) who demonstrated that the rate of productivity growth could be identified with the rate of Hicks-Neutral technical change assuming constant returns to scale and competitive markets. The objective was to provide an elementary way of segregating variations in output per head due to technical change from those due to changes in the availability of capital per head and where technical change was defined as a short hand for any kind of shift in the production function.

Another theoretical development made in the area of measurement of productivity was called the Index Number Theory approach to the subject. The unique correspondence between the type of index used to aggregate over inputs and outputs and the structure of the underlying technology was also developed. For example, the Laspeyres indexing procedure was shown to be exact for, or to imply, a linear production function in which all inputs are perfect substitutes in the production process. Similarly, the Tornqvist index implied a homogeneous translog production function (Cowing and Stevenson, 1981).

The Cost Function model based upon Duality Theory (Denny *et al.*, 1981, Nadiri *et al,* 1981) and the early work of Shephard (1953, 1970) could also be used for measuring Total Factor Productivity where the required assumptions of exogenous output and input prices and cost minimizing behaviour were tenable. The model could also be used to relate such technological characteristics as scale economies, input substitution, and technical change to observed changes in TFP.

Paralleling these theoretical developments in Production Functions and Duality Theory was the development of the related concept of measurement of efficiency in the pioneering work of Farrell (1957) who emphasized that productivity varies not only due to differences in production technology but also due to differences in efficiency of the production process. There could be differences between the observed and the optimal value where the optimality could be expressed in terms of maximum output or minimum input or some behavioural goal of the organization. The comparison can take the form of the ratio of observed output to maximum obtainable output from a given set of inputs, or ratio of minimum obtainable to observed input required to produce the given output. In both these comparisons the optimum is defined in terms of production possibilities and the efficiency concept involved here is referred to as Technical Efficiency. According to Farrell (1957), total efficiency can be decomposed into two parts: Technical Efficiency (T.E.) and Allocative Efficiency (A.E.). T.E. is defined as the ratio of output to maximum output that can be produced from a given set of inputs. This is the output-oriented measure of T.E. The input-oriented measure of T.E. is the ratio of inputs to minimum inputs needed to produce a certain volume of outputs. A.E. is defined as the efficiency measured in the context of use of several inputs in optimal proportions, given input and output prices. T.E. is represented by the distance from the efficient frontier, which means the frontier is a maximum production limit. When the optimum is defined in terms of minimum cost or maximum revenue or maximum profit, there could be definitions of cost efficiency, revenue efficiency and profit efficiency respectively. The measurement of the concept of efficiency necessitated the need for a concept of maximality or frontier in terms of a Frontier Production Function or a Cost Frontier or a Revenue Frontier, etc. A whole set of papers developed in the literature in this direction for measurement of frontiers (Aigner *et al.,* 1977, Schmidt *et al.,* 1979, Bauer, 1990).

Farrell (1957) suggested that one could usefully analyze technical efficiency in terms of realized deviations from an idealized, frontier isoquant provided the frontier is known. Since the production frontier is never known in practice, he suggested that the function be estimated from sample data using either a non-parametric piece-wise linear technology or a parametric one using the Cobb-Douglas function. While the former approach was taken up and developed by Charnes *et al.* (1978) which resulted in the development of the Data Envelopment Analysis (DEA) approach, the latter was taken up by Aigner *et al.,* (1977) resulting in the development of the Stochastic Frontier Method (SFM).

Data Envelopment Analysis uses linear programming to wrap a quasi-convex hull around the data in very much the same way as Farrell's built up the efficient isoquant in which deviations from the frontier provide a measure of relative inefficiency. With quantities and price data, economic efficiency could be calculated and decomposed into its technical and allocative components. Extensions of this basic DEA technique appeared in the literature later (Banker *et al.,* 1986) for handling different types of models consisting of such variables which reflected the presence/absence of a particular facility, variables over which the decision making unit may have no control or where ancillary managerial information needed to be incorporated into the analysis. Its empirical orientation and absence of *a priori* assumptions have resulted in its widespread use in studies involving non-profit organizations such as hospitals, regulated utilities, etc. However, by lumping noise with inefficiency it overestimates inefficiency.

Deprins *et al.* (1984) introduced the concept of the free disposal hull (FDH) in the literature that relaxes the convexity assumption of DEA. FDH envelops the data more tightly than the DEA. Whereas a frontier in the FDH may be dominated by a single observed efficient producer, a producer in the DEA may be dominated by a fictitious observation defined as a linear/convex combination of a set of efficient producers.

The econometric or parametric approach to measurement of efficiency separates noise from estimates of efficiency. But being parametric it confounds the effects of misspecification of functional form (of both technology and inefficiency) with inefficiency. Such a misspecification can occur in the functional form representing technology or can also occur in the functional form used for regressing the inefficiency on its explanatory variables. In early applications (Aigner *et al.,* 1968), a strict interpretation of Farrell's (1957) propositions produced 'deterministic frontiers' embedding errors and stochastic variations in the dependent variable in the inefficiency term. Aigner *et al.* (1977) suggested a more flexible stochastic frontier model in which the two components were specified—one representing stochastic variation having a normal distribution and the other representing inefficiency having a half-normal distribution. Estimation of inefficiency based on other specifications have also been considered in the literature such as use of a truncated-normal distribution by Stevenson (1980), a gamma distribution by Greene (1990), etc.

Schmidt *et al.* (1979) extended the analysis of Aigner *et al.* (1977) by considering the duality between the stochastic frontier production and cost function to measure both technical and allocative efficiency. Where duality may not be identifiable, the cost function needs to be estimated directly. But cost frontier estimation would overstate technical inefficiency if failure to minimize costs is also because of allocative inefficiency considerations. There is, therefore, a need to estimate allocative inefficiency along with technical inefficiency in case of a cost function. Moreover, to increase the efficiency of parametric estimates, a system of equations comprising the cost function and first order conditions of cost minimization (input demand equations) is estimated. But the estimation of this system is problematic because allocative inefficiency element appearing in the cost function equation would always be one-sided (positive), whereas in the first order condition equation, that is, in the input demand equation, it may be positive if an input is over-utilised, or it may be negative if an input is under-utlised. To overcome this problem of estimation of the system of equations, the allocative inefficiency term appearing in the cost function is assumed to be independent of that appearing in the first order condition equations. This is an unrealistic assumption because the allocative inefficiency term appearing in the demand equation is related to allocative inefficiency term shown in the cost function. Thus, what is required to be done is that the allocative inefficiency term appearing in a set of first order conditions (demand equations) be properly integrated with that appearing in the cost frontier. The use of panel data opened up numerous interesting possibilities, providing consistent estimators of inefficiency. Eventually, the assumption of fixed inefficiencies overtime was also relaxed and several models of time-varying inefficiency also appeared in the literature (Cornwell *et al.*, 1990).

Effects of scale economies were also examined with a full blown model of productivity change decomposed into movements along a cost frontier (scale economies), shifts in the cost frontier (technical change), and non-marginal cost pricing developed by Denny *et al.* (1981) and Gollop and Roberts (1981). Denny *et al.* (1981) defined aggregate output growth using both cost elasticities and revenue shares and showed that in the case of marginal cost pricing the two aggregate output growth would be the same. But in case price is different from marginal cost then the output growth represented by revenue share would be different from that given by the cost elasticity share. This difference in output growth arising out of non-marginal cost pricing appears as one of the components of total factor productivity growth. Thus the non-marginal cost pricing component arises because of the way in which output growth has been defined by Denny *et al.* (1981) rather than having any economic meaning in terms of reasons due to resource allocation.

Until now, efficiency of a firm seemed to be considered essentially as an inherently residual concept. Schmidt (1985) observed that when the effects of differences in certain measured inputs are removed, some firms still produce more or less than others which is called inefficiency. The accuracy of the measure would depend on the completeness of the model. For example, not including a variable in the production function such as disaggregated labour input may typically have an effect on efficiency measures. Nevertheless, inefficiency does exist in the real world because of the manner in which inputs are converted into outputs and over which the management has no control. Thus, efficiency change does produce an independent contribution to productivity change. It is, therefore, desirable to incorporate the possibility of efficiency change into models of productivity change. This is the frontier approach to the measurement of productivity. TFP, in this approach, is then defined as the net effect of changes in inefficiency, movement along the frontier (scale economies), and shifts in the frontier, the latter being technical change.

Nishimizu and Page (1982) attempted to incorporate efficiency change into a model of productivity change by decomposing productivity growth into shifts in the production frontier and movements towards or away from it. Caves *et al.* (1982) adopted the input quantity index (defined as ratios of distance functions) introduced by Malmquist in the context of consumer theory to measure firm specific productivity indexes. Termed the Malmquist Productivity Index (MPI), this approach, which is based on ratios of distance functions, is a natural way of modelling the frontier as well as deviations and shifts in that frontier. The distance function and the Malmquist Productivity Index have been discussed in detail in the next Chapter on Methodology of the Study.

2.2 Sectoral Insights

Public utilities such as the railways, electric companies, post offices have multiple outputs. To study technical efficiency, it would require aggregating these outputs into a single index of output. One way of doing this is by using prices which would, in turn, require that output prices are observable and reflect revenue-maximizing behaviour. However, in the case of public utilities such as railways, post offices, this assumption may not hold because of need to cater to other objectives such as full employment, welfare maximization, etc. A better option, therefore, would be to use the distance function approach which requires no such restriction.

Coelli and Perelman (1996) applied this approach to measure technical efficiency of 17 European Railway companies using annual data for the period 1979-83. The distance function was approximated by a translog function and the Corrected Ordinary Least Squares (COLS) method was used for estimation. Outputs were taken as passenger services and freight services performed, while inputs were labour, energy, and capital. TE was also calculated using total revenue of railways transportation obtained by adding revenues from passenger and freight services, and Tornqvist output index using revenue shares to provide weights to passenger and freight activities. The results of the revenue model were vastly different from the other sets of results, with correlation coefficient between the revenue model and others to be as low as 0.178, while correlations amongst the remaining sets ranged from 0.469 to 0.967. The mean TE from revenue model which was 0.536 was substantially lower than others which were of the order of 0.8 to 0.9. It revealed that the use of total revenue as a measure of aggregate output in empirical analysis appeared to be less than satisfactory, confirming the presumption that few publicly owned rail organizations set output prices with market conditions or cost recovery in mind. The study also showed that the choice of orientation of the model was not crucial since input distance function results were found similar to the output distance function results, with correlation coefficient between TE predictions from the two models being as high as 0.967.

Another study showed not much difference in the TEs obtained using the various methods: correlation coefficients between the parametric methods were 0.760 or more (Coelli and Perelman, 1996, 1999). Coelli and Perelman (2000) also studied technical efficiency change, technical progress change, and total factor productivity of the 17 European Railway companies, using data for the period 1979-83 and 1988-93. The results confirmed significant catching up with average TFP growth increasing by 16.7 per cent over this period. Most of this growth in almost all countries took place due to cuts in input usage in staff, rolling stock, and lines during the 1980s. However, as the labour element tends to be sticky downwards, the presumption that it would have been easier for railways to change the usage of input factors may not always be realistic.

Efficiency change has been found to be playing a major role in productivity growth. Analysis of productivity growth (Fare *et al.*, 1990) in Illinois electric utilities for a sample of 19 coal-fired steam electric generating plants for the period 1975-81 using Malmquist Productivity Index (MPI) showed considerable variations in changes in both efficiency and technology, with efficiency change playing a major role in productivity growth. The results suggested that neglecting technical efficiency in the analysis of productivity growth may lead to inappropriate conclusions. In fact, efficiency change as a major source of change was found in 45 out of 108 observations in the sample, as compared to technical change in 31 of the observations.

Output distance function approach was also used to estimate MPI of (Spanish) insurance companies (Fuentes *et al.*, 2001). The data base was built from two sources for the period 1987-94 having 532 observations with three output variables and two input variables. Technical progress was defined in the usual form as a trend variable. A parametric distance function was estimated using the translog functional form for the transformation function and ML method was used for estimation purpose. Efficiency change was measured as ratio of two successive distance functions, and technical change and its components were evaluated using the estimated parameters. TE was significant and was higher than the deterministic case because in the stochastic model part of the deviations is inputted to white noise. MPI was around 1.00 indicating no productivity which conforms to results obtained elsewhere for financial services.

"Inverse" production function has also been used to measure productivity and efficiency of organizations having multiple outputs. Bjurek *et al.* (1990) applied this to analyse the efficiency of 400 social insurance offices of Sweden for the period 1974-84 using one input, labour, and four outputs, namely, income evaluation assessments, sickness reports and control, reimbursements of expenses on medicine, etc., and pension and social insurance payments. This inverse function was justified on the ground that labour costs amount to about 80 per cent of the total costs, and further that other inputs such as capital in the form of office space and computer terminals is almost proportional to labour input and varies very little across offices due to common standards. Efficiency was found to be around 0.80.

This method of circumventing the problem of multiple outputs was used in postal sector by Bradley and Colvin (1999) while studying technical change and productivity in mail processing in the United States Postal Service. A single input, labour, was used as endogenous input which was justified on the ground that labour represented 89 per cent of the mail processing cost and also because there was no sustainable trend in the capital labour ratio which remained at a fairly low level (as was followed by Bjurek *et al.*, 1990 for Swedish insurance companies). The Input Requirement Function was approximated with a translog function. Three output variables, i.e., number of pieces of manual letters sorted, mechanized letters sorted and automated letters sorted were used as regressors, along with a time trend to capture technical change. Data for the period 1988-96 from 250 Postal Service plants in which mail processing took place was used for the estimation. Results showed that mail processing was subject to substantial returns to scale with elasticity of labour with respect to output being substantially less than 1. It also revealed that postal service benefited from technical progress and restructuring in terms of methods of production and revision of work rules which took place in 1993.

Pimenta *et al.* (2000) studied technical efficiency in regard to Portugal's postal services using the same framework, i.e., an Input Requirement Frontier (IRF). Use of IRF was justified on the ground that labour dominates other inputs in the provision of numerous outputs. 22 Public Postal Operators (PPOs) from OECD countries were taken. Data supplied by UPU and supplemented by the operators in response to a questionnaire were used. The stochastic frontier model was estimated by a translog function using 187 observations. The technical efficiency parameters indicated that policy of maintaining an extensive network of counters as part of the universal service obligation resulted in losses in technical efficiency for those operators whose financial services were not representative. Size of the Postal Administration (measured by the number of letter post items), density of delivered objects per delivery point, etc. were some of the variables having favourable impact on technical efficiency. The delivery function of 12 postal administrations was also studied using a similar translog function with labour as the endogenous variable.

Both the above studies are based on the presumption that labour which is the dominant input in postal service is sufficiently variable so as to classify it as an endogenous input. However, labour in postal service is very sticky downwards, being tightly controlled by unions and thus there is hardly any freedom to the managers to adjust this input in response to changes in output.

Standard production function using single output, multiple input was used for studying the productivity and technical efficiency in Postal Services. Perelman and Pesteau (1988) applied this method on a sample of observations of 19 railroads over the period 1970-83, and 21 postal companies for the period 1975-84. In the case of railroads, the two outputs, passengers and freight, were aggregated using an index to make a single aggregate output as the dependent variable. For postal services, only one output, i.e., mailing was taken because the share of financial services was found to be very small. The inputs were labour, structure and equipment. The transformation function used was a translog function estimated by Corrected Ordinary Least Squares (COLS) developed by Greene (1980). In the case of postal services, technical progress was found to be close to zero so that the total factor productivity and efficiency change coincided. Efficiency was explained by Ordinary Least Squares (OLS) regression (log linear) on four exogenous factors: (i) index of tendering which was defined as the ratio of Post offices managed by the private sectors; (ii) ratio of financial activities to mailing services; (iii) number of mailing boxes per capita; (iv) index of regulation, constructed on the basis of response given by each country to a UPU (Universal Postal Union) survey. The study was too limited in its scope as it was restricted to only one output.

Another study in which the model had one output was that by Perelman and Pesteau (1994). Technical efficiencies of 16 national postal services of OECD industrial countries for the period 1975-89 was estimated using one output y as the number of items mailed plus financial services (number of operations) and three inputs: x_l as the total number of employees in full-time units, x_q as equipment (the number of postal vehicles used as a proxy), x_k as capital which is postal offices in activity. The transformation function used was a translog one which was estimated by parametric Stochastic Method introduced by Aigner *et al.* (1977) where V_{it} was a random term distributed as a N $(0, \sigma^2)$ and U_{it} was an efficiency term assumed to be non-negative, uncorrelated with v_{it}, and to follow a half-normal distribution. The result showed a 2.2 per cent shift of the production frontier each year (may be due to introduction of letter sorting machines, etc). There were increasing returns to scale ($\beta_l + \beta q + \beta_k = 0.541+0.167+0.378=1.086$). Most of the variance of the residual term concerned technical efficiency $[\sigma^2_u /(\sigma^2_u + \sigma^2 v) = 0.946]$. Average technical efficiency over 15 years ranged from 0.924 in Netherland to miserable 0.151 for Finland. Estimates of efficiency so obtained were regressed on four exogenous factors: mail box density; inhabitants per mail box; ratio of post offices managed by private sector; and extent of regulatory autonomy. The residuals obtained in this regression were taken to be indicative of management efficiency, the most efficient being the country with the maximum residual. The indicators of managerial efficiency gave a different ranking of countries than that was obtained earlier. Luxembourg and Sweden overtook Netherlands and the UK. As financial services and mailing items are not homogeneous products, and are, in fact, too diverse by nature, their aggregation into one output for the purpose of the study was unrealistic.

Maruyama and Nakajima (2002) measured both productivity and efficiency of postal services in advanced industrialized countries (17 European countries, USA, Australia, and Japan) using an input-oriented model. This was justified on the premise that input variables such as the number of employees and post offices could be controlled by the organization, as compared to the output such as the number of mail items which are uncontrollable demand factors (exogenous) to postal administrations. Data for 20 Postal administrations available in UPU postal statistics for the period 1991-97 were used and supplemented by data from annual reports and other sources. Amongst several inputs used in the post offices, the following were taken: (i) number of full time postal staff; (ii) number of post offices, which was applied as a proxy for capital stock investment; (iii) number of trucks and automobiles as a proxy for raw materials. As the cost of labour represents approximately 70 per cent share of total costs, the representation of inputs was found to be adequate. Three cases were considered. Case I took output as mail items, registered, and express mails, but excluded parcels and international mails. Case II considered number of mails delivered at home. Case III considered real postal receipts. Data Envelopment Analysis (DEA) using Tim Coelli's DEAP version 2.1 was used to measure Malmquist Productivity Index as a product of change in technical efficiency and technical progress. Variable returns to scale technology was assumed for estimating technical efficiency because of significant scale differences among operations and because postal administrations have difficulty in changing their scale of operations promptly. The average technical efficiency in all cases revealed an increasing trend from 0.6 in case I to 0.7 in case III. Japan and US showed TE = 1 for all three cases. Result in case III exceeds the average of both cases I and II, which can be attributed to the impact of output factors (parcels, international mails) that were not included in other cases. The average value of MPI (Malmquist Productivity Index) displayed similar trends.

The factors affecting technical efficiency were studied on the basis of a regression with postal items per capita, population per square km, and management structure as explanatory variables. Tobit estimation was carried out by taking log of TE indicators and then using Generalized Least Squares method. Postal demand and delivery route density as represented by postal items per capita and population per square km were found to have positive effect on efficiency, as also the management structure. The results were found to be consistent with other studies. Though quite comprehensive in choice of inputs it excluded parcels and international mails which are important products in an era of e-commerce and globalization. Moreover, using an input-oriented model on the premise that input variables such as number of employees can be controlled by the organization is not, as mentioned earlier, a very realistic proposition. Also, in the presence of non-constant returns to scale, the MPI does not accurately measure productivity change. As shown by Grifell-Tatje, Lovell (1995) MPI overstates true productivity change when input growth occurred in the presence of decreasing returns to scale and understates productivity change when input growth occurred in the presence of increasing returns to scale. There is, therefore, a need for an additional term to account for the scale effect in cases where it may be considered important.

Deprins *et al.* (1984) used a different method to measure the labour efficiency in 792 post offices in Belgium (and found an estimated labour efficiency of about 90%). One input, namely, labour and six broad aggregations of outputs, namely, financial operations, registered mail, special delivery mail, unaddressed printed matter, outgoing mail, and delivery points (out of 137 categories of items handled or operations performed) were used. The method used by Farrell (1957), i.e., convexification of the data set was found to be unwarranted. The method found most appropriate was to infer a set of efficient points consisting of only those points that carry more output with same inputs, or same output with fewer inputs. This method requires a simple comparison of input and output components of the vectors in the data set, so as to locate "dominating" ones.

Cost function was used by Norsworthy *et al.* (1991), i.e. a translog restricted Variable Cost Function to analyse the productivity of Management Sectional Centres (MSC) responsible for the collection, forwarding and delivery of mails in the United States Postal Service. The data base for the study was a cross-section of 200 MSCs for the year 1984, with 8 output categories of deliveries and collected mails and 3 network variables, namely, labour, material, and quasi-fixed capital inputs. The cost function and the input demand equations were estimated simultaneously using the full information maximum likelihood method. The ratio of each of the outputs to the inputs weighted by factor shares were calculated, which were then weighted by their respective marginal costs to arrive at a measure of TFP. Substantial productivity differences were found to exist among the MSCs within regions and size classes, thereby suggesting scope for improvement in particular MSCs and hence of overall system performance. The behavioural assumption of cost-minimization required for proper identification of the model was justified on the ground that the estimated cost function was found to be quasi-concave in input prices (i.e., the factor demand equations were downward-sloping) and that the estimated cost function was found to be monotonically non-decreasing in output (thus showing that the input was moving in the same direction as the output). With regard to the requirement of variability in inputs with respect to input prices it was contended that as the variable input demand function is a function not only of input prices but also of the various output quantities, network served, and capital used, the model need not require any variation whatsoever in prices of variable inputs. The theory of production or the conditions for estimating a cost function-based model do not decree a particular degree of variation in the variable input prices; prices may be identical across firms as long as other variables show sufficient variation to identify the demand equations. What is essential is that prices should appear in the cost function and in the input demand equations. It was further stated that as the estimated input demand equations showed a high value for R-square, it implied that there were no insufficient variation in the determinants of input demand to explain movements in input quantities demanded. Evidently, the assumption of cost minimization would not hold in case of public postal operators as there are competing objectives. Equally important is the fact that input price for labour would not reflect the marginal cost of employing labour as postal employees are paid national wages on the basis of job classification and seniority. For these reasons, the estimated cost function would tell us nothing about the productivity of the system.

For Indian Postal Department, Jha *et al.* (1990) estimated the efficiency (in fact, productivity) for the period from 1950-51 to 1983-84. Revenue at constant prices was estimated by correcting the revenue for index numbers of regulated prices. These corrected figures were taken to be approximately reflecting the output. By dividing these figures by price of a postcard in the year 1950-51, estimates of postal services in postcard equivalents were obtained which were comparable over time. The resource cost was also estimated at constant prices and productive efficiency was obtained by dividing the estimates of postcard equivalent of total revenue by the total economic cost. Thereafter, an index of economic efficiency was calculated with 1950-51 as base year. Estimates revealed a fall in productivity in the 1950s with a gradual rise in the beginning of the 1960s. The index of productivity was 1.19 in 1983-84, reaching a high of 1.29 in the year 1979-80. Increasing returns to scale was also indicated as elasticity of cost with respect to output was found to be 0.616, thereby implying that inefficiency, if any, was one of scale inefficiency which decreased in the 1960s. However, the study was inherently deficient in its scope as it used administered prices for aggregating the outputs on the presumption that these prices, like market prices, revealed preferences of the consumers. Empirical analysis have shown that total revenue as a measure of aggregate output appears to be less than satisfactory because few publicly owned organizations set output prices with market conditions or cost recovery in mind (Coelli *et al.*, 2000). As this behavioural assumption of revenue maximization does not hold in case of India Post, the study was of limited use.

2.3 Pricing: A Brief Overview and Some Sectoral Insights

Pricing of postal products/services is a complex subject due to several factors unique to the postal sector. These are: (i) joint production of several products under conditions of economies of scale and scope, (ii) absence of a single aggregate cost function, (iii) conceptual difficulties in defining and measuring marginal cost, and (iv) Universal Service Obligation (USO). Because of the joint production of several products under conditions of economies of scale in an unregulated market, it may lead to monopoly prices which are Pareto inefficient. Under such a condition, the Pareto efficient price was derived by Faulhaber (1975) which is the cross-subsidy free price.

Absence of a single aggregate cost function emanates from the fact that a variety of products are offered by postal administrations using different technologies in various stages of operations, from posting of mail to its delivery. Product costing is, therefore, done at the functional level. The production technologies in the cost pool segments are represented by different transformation functions: translog for estimating mail processing labour and transportation costs; constant elasticity for retail (window services) costs, etc. Further, as there is no unique relationship between costs and volume of products, the cost function is related to volume through cost drivers (cost causative characteristics such as cubic-foot miles in case of transport, for example). Estimation of a cost function as also measuring marginal cost becomes difficult.

Marginal cost can at best be defined as average cost obtained by dividing the product of cost component, elasticity of cost driver, and distribution key share, by volume, and summing this across cost components (Unit Volume Variable Cost). The amount of driver, cost pool elasticities and other parameters are calculated from econometric studies, expert opinion, sampling, engineering or simulation models, benchmarking from other postal administrations. Discrete changes in cost driver levels are used to give measure of incremental costs. The incremental cost for a particular product is the sum of all component costs arrived at by calculating the driver cost of each component on the basis of its elasticity and deducting the driver cost of all other products except the one whose incremental cost is being measured. The component costs for each product are added assuming additive separability (which also implicitly assumes that all variations are explained by cost drivers and that the relationship between cost component and cost driver remains stable). In this way the overall cost is estimated for the postal service as a whole. The marginal cost and the average incremental cost would be the same if cost function is linear and there are no product specific costs. In case of economies of scale the marginal cost so calculated needs to be adjusted downwards.

Bradley *et al.* (1999) found that in the case of the U.S. postal system, the costing system disaggregates functional costs for mail processing, transportation, delivery and other components into 19 different "cost segments", with over 500 different further sub-divisions into cost-components/pools. The aggregate enterprise cost surface is often approximated at the macro level by a simple constant functional form, whose parameters are taken from the micro-level relationships evaluated at output forecast levels. The two approaches, macro and micro, would give different estimates because of differences in functional forms. The constant elasticity functional form is used in case of the macro approach and the translog form in the case of the micro approach. The first order term in the translog is the elasticity and so if the second order term is large then there will be a difference between the two estimates. The second order term will be large if there are still economies of scale to be exploited. In the U.S. postal system, economies of scale are largely exhausted and hence the differences in costs between the two approaches are small. The estimates would also differ if there are multiple drivers that affect component costs and also when the relative amounts of the driver are in unequal proportions as in delivery of mails where different shapes act as different cost drivers in the casing of a carrier's mail.

Micro approaches are more precise but require substantial amount of additional detailed work. It should, therefore, be used for the purposes of rate-making where even a small error in the incremental costs of competitive products could have meaningful consequences for the competing firms. If the incremental costs are required for financial planning or to perform scenario analyses then the macro approach, which is more general, would suffice.

Activity Based Costing (ABC) has also been tried out in some postal administrations including United States Postal Service because of its advantages over the traditional costing system in focusing on overheads. The fixed costs are defined and understood and efforts are made to trace them to products in proportion to how each product "consumes" these activities. Thus, because of a high level of common costs and the wide range of postal products, ABC would be particularly useful for postal administrations by tracing more of common costs through activities to different products (Awerbuch *et al.*, 2000).

A feature which is unique to the issues relating to pricing of postal products is the need to consider the Universal Service Obligation (USO) of postal administrations. As per Universal Postal Convention, Universal Postal Service is defined as the permanent provision of quality basic postal services at all points in a member country's territory, for all customers, at affordable prices. USO can be defined not only by product but also by activity. The product definition focuses on the core letter product that is delivered throughout the country at a uniform rate and the activity definition usually focuses on an activity like delivery that the administration must provide although it does so at a loss. As under USO, the service is generally being provided at a loss, it is made good by profits elsewhere. There is, therefore, a need to measure the Cost of Universal Service (COUS) which needs to be factored into pricing decisions. COUS can be calculated either by the Net Avoided Cost method (NAC) or by the Entry Pricing method (EP). The NAC method, initially used in telecommunications, is calculated as the net total of financial gains cumulatively available from (notional) withdrawal of loss-making routes.

For the activity definition, NAC is simply the difference between the revenue and the costs of the deficit routes calculated for all the products, i.e., both monopoly products and the competitive products. The logic is that the postal operator is incurring losses in the current environment on all the mail delivered on deficit routes and it could increase its profits by simply ceasing to provide service to customers on these routes. The NAC method for product definition is the difference between the cost of providing the monopoly product and its revenue on the deficit routes. This would be greater (or less) than the activity measure if the revenue from the competitive products exceed (or is exceeded by) their stand alone costs. Bradley and Colvin (2001) observed that much of the delivery costs are fixed and would remain so even if the monopoly product was withdrawn from the deficit areas and suggest that as such NAC should only be the difference between the monopoly products' revenue and their incremental costs on the deficit route.

The NAC method implicitly assumes the market structure to be stable. But in an era of liberalization, entry of competitors in the market may cause drop in revenue of the incumbent operator because of a lower price being charged by the entrant not only due to its lower cost, but also because the existing incumbent may be charging a higher price to finance the loss being incurred on account of its USO. Profitable services can be skimmed away and the resulting loss of market share for the incumbent will raise the cost of the USO as the incumbent loses its scale and scope advantages. This brings to the forefront the concept of calculating the COUS by the EP method.

The cost of the USO under the EP method is measured by the sum of the losses of revenue to the incumbent on each of the routes where entry occurs less the impact on the incumbent's costs. Thus, under the EP method, there is not a single cost of the USO as under NAC but one which depends on the liberalization being proposed and evaluated. The EP approach to the activity definition is the loss in revenue in both the monopoly and the competitive product due to the liberalization of the market. The product definition is the loss in contribution from the monopoly product on surplus routes, i.e., it is the difference between the revenue and cost of the monopoly product on the surplus routes as these are the only volumes lost by the incumbent. It will be smaller than the activity measure if the revenue from the competitive product is greater than its stand alone delivery and up-stream costs.

Rodriguez *et al.* (1999) while estimating the cost of the Universal Service Obligation (USO) using the EP method found the estimates by the two methods to be totally different, in fact, reverse. This is because a low estimate of the cost of the USO under NAC implies few loss-making routes thus offering potential for profitable entry on many routes. As entry on a large scale is likely to occur in such a scenario on these routes being opened for competition, a high cost of the USO would be estimated under entry pricing from volume loss and the accompanying drop in contribution. This would further undermine the incumbent's ability to support the fixed costs of the network thereby increasing the number of loss-making routes (as a result of a rise in average incremental costs in response to the loss of economies of scale and scope) from that found at the pre-liberalization uniform price.

The EP method is more appropriate as this is the universal cost most closely associated with "cream-skimming". Clearly the monopoly product on the surplus route is where the "cream" is in terms of total profit. Liberalization that would allow cream skimming thus imposes the largest cost of universal obligation on the operator. In case of an earlier break-even situation, now the incumbent would be required to raise the prices on the competitive products which would lead to a graveyard spiral of falling market share and increasing losses. From a public policy perspective, therefore, this is an important conclusion for if a financial cost measure is used to evaluate the cost of the USO, the results of a calculation based on net avoided cost will be misleading to policy makers as they will understate the effect of large scale liberalization on the financial viability of the incumbent operator.

Costing of postal products has also been tried using the telecommunication model. Soares *et al.* (2002) has explored this possibility because of a similarity between a telecommunication network and a postal network. The access network in the case of a postal network with delivery to and collection from delivery offices resembles closely the telephone network, access circuit where the sorting centres are equivalent to the switches and the inter-sorting transport routes are equivalent to the trunking circuit network. Indeed there are some differences too. The postal network is asymmetric because there is a separate collection and delivery network unlike the telecommunication network.

Pricing decisions need to take into account other factors affecting the cost of delivery of mails. Roy (1999) has shown that, apart from the traffic and density of delivery points, the grouping index defined as the vertical concentration of houses in a building is also one of the main costs factor affecting delivery. Scarfiglieri *et al.* (2001) found that postal density which is the total number of households and firms per postal route is much more important than number of mails per drop (proxied by income) as a driver of postal costs and profitability. These have implications for charging lower prices in urban areas. Cazals *et al.* (2001) through the use of a translog cost function for analyzing the effect of size of mails on the cost of out door delivery showed that the marginal costs of the non-standard, parcel, and other mails were approximately 2, 21, and 17 times that of the standard size letters. The overall cost elasticity showed increasing returns to scale.

The cost-recovery regulation framework which existed earlier throughout the industrialized world to regulate industries never found favour in postal administrations. What gained popularity was the Price-Cap Regulation (PCR) both in the telecommunications industry in the 1980s as a replacement for cost recovery regulation as well as in many advanced postal administrations such as Germany, U.K., Australia, Canada, New Zealand, etc. Under PCR, a firm is allowed to increase prices at a rate not exceeding inflation minus an adjustment factor. When properly formulated, price-caps can promote efficiency gains and increase pricing flexibility and simplicity. Its operation requires a decision on the products which are to be covered under this regulation. Treworgy *et al.* (1999) has made an international comparison and assessment of PCR in the postal sector. Whereas, Netherlands included almost all the services within USO, New Zealand, Australia, and Canada included only basic letters. Thus there is no fixed definition of the product basket which and would vary from one administration to another.

As competition is generally believed to lead to efficiency, one way of ensuring this in the postal sector is through a pricing decision incorporating features of work sharing. It is a kind of unbundling of processes which are then open to competition. The work sharing notion is that a discount is offered to mailers or competitors who do perform a portion of the postal work and then turn the mail over to postal service for completion of delivery. The discount should not be based entirely on avoided costs. If not properly regulated it may adversely affect the incumbent posts as the presence of nation-wide averaged prices may lead to a situation where granting of access can facilitate wasteful, cream-skimming entry. Entrants can exploit the Postal system's responsibility to serve as a carrier of last resort in high cost regions and operate in lucrative areas to engage in profitable "cream-skimming". This may lead to a situation where the incumbent post would have to resort to increase in prices to sustain the USO and cause a "graveyard spiral" of increasing prices and decreasing market share.

Where postal services are priced below cost, then the pricing rule given by Panzar (2002) is that the appropriate price ceiling on the unbundled access rate should be equal to the stamp price less per unit postal costs saved so long as this is not below postal average incremental costs of access. That is, instead of a price ceiling in case of subsidy-free pricing, now there is a price floor for access. This is the same as the Delivery-Area Access Pricing or DAP, as given by Crew and Kleindorfer (2002), which states that entrants who by-pass upstream operations of the post office should not be charged according to the work they have by-passed, but according to the work yet to be performed in delivering the mail they repost with the post office. The access policy can also be based on the sub-class price arrived at by attributing costs and using a mark up to arrive at the price of the by-passed stages in deciding the discount. That is, it should be per unit marginal cost of service plus any foregone profit on the diverted volume (Pickett *et al.,* 2000). Such a policy can also lead to a Pareto Optimal situation as shown by Mitchell (1999) where the work done by the mailer is at a lower cost than that done by the postal sector, and the consequent cost savings of the postal sector leading to a higher profit. The postal service is better off with no mailer being worse off and the money can be used to lower prices for all mailers.

2.4 Issues

Review of the relevant literature shows that considerable work has been done on estimating productivity and efficiency of postal administrations in advanced industrialized countries of Europe, USA, Australia, and Japan but no such attempts have been undertaken in the context of developing economies like India. The study undertaken by Jha *et al.* (1990) on India Post was too limited in its scope. As mentioned earlier, it used revenue as a basis for measuring output. Aggregating multiple outputs into a single index of output using prices is an adequate representation provided prices are market determined so as to reveal the preferences of the consumers. It also requires the behavioural assumption of revenue maximization on the part of the producers. Empirical analysis have shown that total revenue as a measure of aggregate output appears to be less than satisfactory because few publicly owned organizations set output prices with market conditions or cost recovery in mind (Coelli *et al.,* 2000). As these conditions do not hold in case of India Post, the study was inherently deficient in its objective of measuring productivity (efficiency). Thus, a study on productivity and efficiency of the postal sector in the Indian context should be based on the quantity of outputs rather than their prices.

Bradley *et al.* (1999), Pimenta *et al.* (2000) circumvented the problem of multiple outputs/multiple inputs in case of postal services by the use of an IRF or an "inverse" production function using a single dominant input labour and multiple outputs. The IRF do summarize multiple outputs, single input technology, giving the minimal amount of labour input required to produce the vector of outputs. One could justify this by arguing that the level of demand for postal products is determined by demographic and macro-economic factors. Postal operators are, therefore, obliged to supply the required quantity of services being determined exogenously, and are only able to control inputs. However, this presumption does not hold in reality. Labour, the most dominant input in the post office, is very sticky downwards, being tightly controlled by the union movement with hardly any freedom to the managers to adjust labour in response to changes in the exogenous variables such as output. On the contrary, post offices have more control over the output quantities *via* price adjustments and advertising, than over their input quantities, especially, labour. The use of an IRF version of the production function model for estimating technical efficiency, as has been done in some studies is, therefore, not appropriate. A logical corollary is that labour should not appear as an endogenous variable in a study on productivity and efficiency of the postal sector and that an output oriented model would be more suitable.

Modelling a technology using a dual cost function would be most appropriate for studying the productivity and efficiency of the organization having multiple outputs and inputs. But this requires the assumption of cost-minimization which does not hold for India Post. Being a Department of the Government of India, it has a set of competing objectives, e.g., universal daily service, convenient locations, speedy delivery, low cost, etc. The Postal management is thus faced with several priorities and does not pursue the objective of cost-minimization which is needed for estimating a cost frontier required for studying productivity and efficiency. Even if the estimated factor demand function is downward sloping, this in no sense "proves" cost minimization, as was argued by Norsworthy *et al.* (1991). This is because there could be large differences between downward-sloped and having the optimal slope. Quasi-concavity is a necessary, but not sufficient condition for cost-minimization. At best, the estimated cost function can be construed as an "institutional" cost function, expressing current practices, which may be established through union rules, standardized business practices or other managerial guidelines.

Moreover, in using a cost function, behaviour of prices of input is important in the sense that they should reflect marginal cost. In the case of postal services, the key input is labour and, therefore, its prices would play a critical role. Labour price should reflect the marginal cost of using additional labour of that type. However, as postal employees are paid national wages on the basis of job classification and seniority with step increases, the variable would be representing an average wage instead of marginal cost. Further, with high retention rates, the ability of managers to adjust labour in response to changes in relative prices seems very limited. As a result, it would not be clear as to what the estimated "factor" demand equations would convey. Also, as all coefficients would be estimated simultaneously, difficulties with the labour price variable may contaminate estimates of other parameters. A high R-square, if obtained, may indicate measurement problems, with errors occurring on both sides of the equations rather than explaining high proportion of observed variation. The estimated cost function would, therefore, tell us almost nothing about the costs or productivity of the system as a whole. The estimates could perhaps conform to managerial practice rather than technical feasibility. There would be no way of determining as to what extent current managerial practice would conform to cost-minimization. For these reasons, findings based on the estimated model of cost function may not reflect economic efficiency. Estimating a cost function for studying productivity and efficiency would, therefore, not give accurate results.

Using the index number approach to measurement of productivity, would also not be applicable in case of public postal operators like India Post as it requires the behavioural assumptions of cost-minimization and revenue-maximization. Moreover, the index number approach assumes all firms to be efficient and therefore, would not sort out technical progress and efficiency.

Normally, any study on postal services must include both multiple outputs and inputs. Review reveals that the choice of output has been too restrictive. For example, Perelman *et al.* (1988) restricted the study to only one output, mailing, on the ground that the share of financial services was found to be very small. In another study by them (Perelman *et al.*, 1994), financial services were added to the mailing items despite the fact these two services/products are not homogeneous so as to justify their aggregation into one output. The study was also limited in its scope as it was confined to only one endogenous output. Even Maruyama's *et al.* (2002) study, though quite comprehensive in choice of inputs, excluded parcels and international mails, which in an era of e-commerce and globalization are not only important items but also have immense potential for growth and therefore, ought to have been considered. The study should, therefore, have been more comprehensive in the sense that it should be based both on multiple-outputs as well as multiple-inputs.

2.5 Summary

From the above analysis, the picture which clearly emerges is that a comprehensive study on productivity and efficiency of India Post is singularly missing and that such a study should incorporate multiple outputs and multiple inputs. Even then some aggregation of products/services would be required, because India Post handles a large number of products. Accordingly, in this study all the postal products/services have been classified under broad categories, taking care that none of the products/services have been omitted. To give completeness to the study, the pricing issues of postal products/services have also been looked into because pricing policy and productivity of the organization are related. It also needs to be emphasized that as India Post is facing diminished reserved areas due to opening of the postal market, higher productivity and efficiency of India Post has become critical for its survival. Competition from private operators in the market has also made pricing issues crucial. Because of these considerations a study on productivity, efficiency, and pricing of India Post was necessitated and has been undertaken. The detailed methodology of the study is spelt out in the next Chapter.

3

Methodology and Data Sources

3.1 Introduction

Measuring the performance of a public utility like postal services is both a complex and difficult task. This is because the objectives according to which the organization needs to be assessed are far too many and often conflicting. Measuring the degree to which the various objectives have been satisfied would entail computing an indicator of performance of each of them and then assigning weightage to those indicators. The only objective for which no extenuating circumstances can be invoked is that of technical efficiency. For any public enterprise not necessarily operating in an environment of monopoly and regulation, the technical efficiency objective, i.e., the maximization of physical outputs for a given combination of physical inputs, is, in fact, the only objective that is compatible with all other objectives of the enterprise. It need not have an objective of profit maximization, cost minimization, or revenue maximization. But it cannot have any logical reason for not pursuing the objective of technical efficiency. For this reason, this appears to be an unavoidable goal.

Measuring productivity and technical efficiency of any organization would be a simple exercise given that the frontier production set is known. As the true production set cannot be found in the blue prints of an engineer, it must be constructed from a sample of possible inefficient operations. That is why one often uses the term "best practice" production set which is made up of those observations that appear to be the best ones in the sense of some posited assumption of dominance. For this reason, the choice of the sample of observations is crucial. It is also important that they originate from similar conditions as to technology and should be such that they may be reasonably construed as operating in the same environment. Keeping in view the above considerations, the study has been confined to the operations of India Post with reference to its counterparts in developing countries only.

3.2 The Approach

From discussions in the previous Chapter, a picture which clearly emerges is to adopt a suitable method for modelling multiple-output, multiple-input technology for productivity and efficiency studies of India Post. The Distance Function approach allows the possibility of specifying a multiple-output, multiple-input technology. It is a natural way of modelling the production frontier as also deviations from and shifts in that frontier, i.e. technical efficiency and technical change. As this approach does not require information on price or behavioural assumptions such as cost minimization/profit maximization, etc., it therefore appears to be an ideal method to be used in studying productivity and efficiency in post offices.

3.2.1 Distance Functions

We begin by noting that the production technology defined by the set, S, may be equivalently defined by the production technology of the firm using the output set, $P(x)$, which represents the set of all output vectors, $\mathbf{y} \in R_+^M$, which can be produced using the input vector, $x \in R_+^K$. That is, $P(x) = \{\mathbf{y} \in R_+^M : \mathbf{x} \text{ can produce } \mathbf{y}\}$.

We assume that the technology satisfies the following axioms. For each **x**, the output set $P(x)$ is assumed to satisfy:

(i) $0 \in P(x)$: nothing can be produced out of a given set of inputs (i.e. inaction is possible);
(ii) non-zero output levels cannot be produced from zero level of inputs;
(iii) $P(x)$ satisfies strong disposability of outputs: if $\mathbf{y} \in P(x)$ and $\mathbf{y}^* \leq \mathbf{y}$ then $\mathbf{y}^* \in P(x)$;
(iv) $P(x)$ satisfies strong disposability of inputs: if $\mathbf{y}$ can be produced from x, then $\mathbf{y}$ can be produced from any $x^* \geq x$;

(v) P($\boldsymbol{x}$) is closed;
(vi) P($\boldsymbol{x}$) is bounded; and
(vii) P($\boldsymbol{x}$) is convex.

Similar assumptions, with the exception of "boundedness", are made regarding the input sets defined for the inputs sets, L(y).

The assumption of closedness is essentially a mathematical requirement but the bounded nature of P($\boldsymbol{x}$) implies that we cannot produce unlimited levels of outputs with a given set of inputs. Convexity implies that if two combinations of output levels can be produced with a given input vector $\boldsymbol{x}$, then any average of these output vectors can also be produced. This assumption implicitly requires the commodities to be continuously divisible.

The output distance function which was introduced by Shephard (1970) is defined on the output set P (x) as:

$$D_0 (\boldsymbol{x}, \mathbf{y}) = \min \{\theta : (\boldsymbol{x}, \mathbf{y}/\theta) \, \varepsilon \, P(\boldsymbol{x})\}$$

D_0 ($\boldsymbol{x}$, **y**) is non-decreasing, positively linearly homogeneous and convex in **y** and decreasing in $\boldsymbol{x}$. The distance function, D_0 ($\boldsymbol{x}$, **y**), will take a value which is less than or equal to one if the output vector **y**, is an element of the feasible production set, P($\boldsymbol{x}$). That is, $D_0 (\boldsymbol{x}, \mathbf{y}) \leq 1$ if $\mathbf{y} \, \varepsilon \, P(\boldsymbol{x})$. Furthermore, the distance function will take a value of unity, if **y** is located on the outer boundary of the production possibility set. That is, $D_0 (\boldsymbol{x}, \mathbf{y}) = 1$ if **y** ε Isoq P($\boldsymbol{x}$) = {$\boldsymbol{x}$, **y**: **y** ε P($\boldsymbol{x}$), ω**y** (does not belong to) ε/P($\boldsymbol{x}$), ω > 1}.

The concept of an output distance function can be illustrated using an example of two outputs, y_1 and y_2 and one input x. The production technology can be represented on a two dimensional diagram as given below in Figure 3.1.

Here the production possibility set, P($\boldsymbol{x}$), is the area bounded by the production possibility frontier, Isoq P($\boldsymbol{x}$), and the y_1 and y_2 axes. The value of the distance function for the point, A = (y_{1a}, y_{2a}), which defines the production point where firm produces $y_{1a,}$ of output 1 and y_{2a} of output 2, using the given quantity of the input, is equal to the ratio θ = OA/OB. This distance is the inverse of the proportion by which the production of all output quantities could be increased while still remaining within the feasible production possibility set for the given input level.

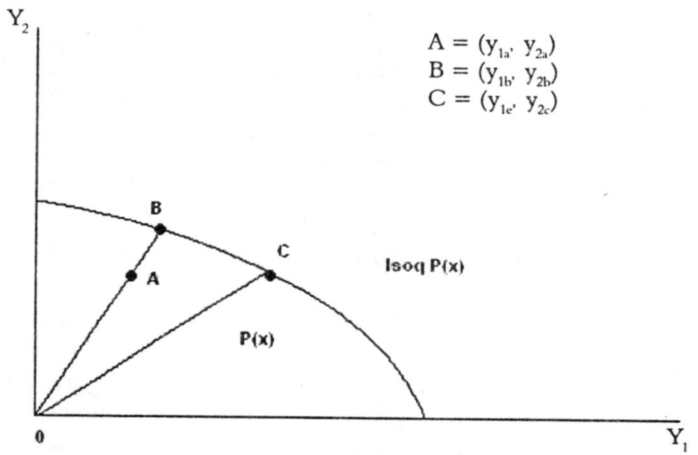

Figure 3.1: Concept of Output Distance Function

This distance measure is the inverse of the Farrell-type output-oriented measure of technical inefficiency. Geometrically, the distance measure, θ, is equal to the ratio OA/OB. The distances OA and OB are radial distances and hence are equal to the Euclidean distances.

$$OA = \|y_a\| = \sqrt{\left(y_{1a}^2 + y_{2a}^2\right)}$$

and

$$OB = \|y_b\| = \sqrt{\left(y_{1b}^2 + y_{2b}^2\right)} \text{ respectively.}$$

Points B and C are on the production possibility surface denoted by Isoq P(x) and, hence, would have distance function values equal to 1.

Similarly, the input distance function can be defined on the input set, L(**y**), as: $D_1(\boldsymbol{x}, \mathbf{y}) = \max\{\, P:(\boldsymbol{y}, \boldsymbol{x}/P) \,\varepsilon\, L(\mathbf{y}) \,\}$, where the input set L(**y**) represents the set of all input vectors, $\boldsymbol{x} \,\varepsilon\, R_+^K$. That is,

$$L(\mathbf{y}) = \left\{\boldsymbol{x} \,\varepsilon\, R_+^K : \boldsymbol{x} \text{ can produce } \boldsymbol{y}\right\}$$

$D_I(x, \mathbf{y})$ is non-decreasing, positively linearly homogeneous and concave in x and increasing, in $\mathbf{y}$. The distance function $D_I(x, \mathbf{y})$ will take a value which is greater than or equal to one if the input vector, x, is an element of the feasible input set, $L(\mathbf{y})$. That is, $D_I(x, \mathbf{y}) \geq 1$ if $x \varepsilon L(\mathbf{y})$. Furthermore, the distance function will take a value of unity if $\mathbf{x}$ is located on the inner boundary of the input set. Technical efficiency is the inverse of the value of the distance function.

3.2.2 *Malmquist Productivity Index*

The Malmquist Productivity Index (MPI) which is constructed from distance functions is used to assess the productivity and efficiency of organisations. It can be estimated by non-parametric and parametric methods. Malmquist firm-specific productivity indexes were introduced by Caves *et al.* (1982). They named these indexes after Malmquist, who had earlier proposed constructing input quantity indexes as ratios of distance functions. Although not recognized by the authors at that time, the formulation of these indexes in terms of distance functions also leads to straightforward calculation by exploiting the relation between distance functions and Farrell measures of technical efficiency.

The Malmquist-type productivity index is potentially very useful in calculating productivity growth in the presence of inefficiency, allowing explicit calculation (and isolation) of changes in efficiency. It does not require price or share data, allowing applications where outputs or inputs may not be marketable. It exploits the fact that the component distance functions are reciprocal to Farrell measures of technical efficiency. Isolation of changes in efficiency and technical change does, however, require panel data.

An orientation of the model-output or input is selected depending on which quantities, inputs or outputs, the managers have most control. For postal sector, an output orientation model is more appropriate as labour which is the most dominant input in post office is very sticky downwards, and the manager, therefore, has very little control over it. On the other hand, post offices have greater control over their output quantities, *via* price adjustments and advertising, than over their input quantities. However, in many instances, the choice of orientation has only a minor influence upon the results obtained (Coelli and Perelman, 1996).

Caves *et al.* (1982) define an output oriented Malmquist Productivity Index between two periods, *t* and *t*+1, using either period *t* technology, or using period *t*+1 technology. This requires a definition of distance functions with respect to two different time periods such as:

$$D_0^t(\mathbf{x}_{t+1},\mathbf{y}_{t+1}) = \min\{\theta:(\mathbf{x}_{t+1},\mathbf{y}_{t+1}/\theta)\varepsilon P(\mathbf{x}_t)\},$$

$$D_0^{t+1}(\mathbf{x}_t,\mathbf{y}_t) = \min\{\theta: (\mathbf{x}_t,\mathbf{y}_t/\theta)\varepsilon P(\mathbf{x}_{t+1})\}$$

The first distance function measures the maximum proportional change in outputs required to make ($x_{t+1,}$ $\mathbf{y}_{t+1}$) feasible in relation to the technology at the previous period *t*. Similarly, the second mixed-period distance function measures the maximum proportional change in output required to make (x_t, $\mathbf{y}_t$) feasible in relation to the technology at *t*+1, which is D_0^{t+1} (x_t, $\mathbf{y}_t$). In both these mixed-period cases, the value of the distance function may exceed unity. This can occur if the observation being evaluated is not feasible in the other period.

An output-oriented MPI using period *t* technology is defined as:

$$M_0^t(\mathbf{y}_t,\mathbf{x}_t,\mathbf{y}_{t+1},\mathbf{x}_{t+1}) = D_0^t(\mathbf{y}_{t+1},\mathbf{x}_{t+1})/D_0^t(\mathbf{y}_t,\mathbf{x}_t)$$

An output-oriented MPI using period t+1 technology can be similarly defined with t+1 substituting for t above as follows:

$$M_0^t(\mathbf{y}_t,\mathbf{x}_t,\mathbf{y}_{t+1},\mathbf{x}_{t+1}) = D_0^{t+1}(\mathbf{y}_{t+1},\mathbf{x}_{t+1})/D_0^{t+1}(\mathbf{y}_t,\mathbf{x}_t)$$

The output oriented MPI focuses on the maximum output that can be produced using a given input vector and a given production technology relative to the observed levels of outputs. It is the minimal output deflation factor such that the deflated output vector for the organisation *i* in period *t*+1, $\mathbf{y}_{t+1}/[\,m_0'(.)]$ and the input vector, $x_{t+1,}$ are just on the production surface of the technology in period *t*. If country *i* has a higher level of productivity than is implied by the period *t* technology, then the MPI > 1.

Instead of measuring the MPI using the period t technology or the period $t+1$ technology and to avoid arbitrariness, it would be more appropriate to take the geometric mean of the MPI obtained using the period t technology and the period $t+1$ technology. Fare *et al.* (1994) has shown that the Malmquist (output oriented) TFP change index between period t (the base period) and period $t+1$ is given by:

$$m_0(\mathbf{y}_{t+1}, \mathbf{x}_{t+1}, \mathbf{y}_t, \mathbf{x}_t) = \left[\left\{D_0^t(\mathbf{y}_{t+1}, \mathbf{x}_{t+1}) / D_0^t(\mathbf{y}_t, \mathbf{x}_t)\right\} \star \left\{D_0^{t+1}(\mathbf{y}_{t+1}, \mathbf{x}_{t+1}) / D_0^{t+1}(\mathbf{y}_t, \mathbf{x}_t)\right\}\right]^{\frac{1}{2}}$$

$$= \frac{D_0^{t+1}(\mathbf{y}_{t+1}, \mathbf{x}_{t+1})}{D_0^t(\mathbf{y}_t, \mathbf{x}_t)} \left[\left\{D_0^t(\mathbf{y}_{t+1}, \mathbf{x}_{t+1}) / D_0^{t+1}(\mathbf{y}_{t+1}, \mathbf{x}_{t+1})\right\} \star \left\{D_0^t(\mathbf{y}_t, \mathbf{x}_t) / D_0^{t+1}(\mathbf{y}_t, \mathbf{x}_t)\right\}\right]^{\frac{1}{2}}$$

where the ratio outside the square bracket measures the change in the output-oriented measure of Farrell technical efficiency between periods t and $t+1$. That is, the efficiency change is equivalent to the ratio of the Farrell technical efficiency in period $t+1$ to the Farrell technical efficiency in period t. The remaining part of the index in the above equation is a measure of technical change. It is the geometric mean of the shift in technology between the two periods, evaluated at the input level x_{t+1} and also at x_t.

$$\text{Efficiency change} = \mathrm{D}_0^{t+1}(\mathbf{y}_{t+1}, \mathbf{x}_{t+1}) / \mathrm{D}_0^t(\mathbf{y}_t, \mathbf{x}_t)$$

$$\text{Technical change} = \left[\left\{\mathrm{D}_0^t(\mathbf{y}_{t+1}, \mathbf{x}_{t+1}) / \mathrm{D}_0^{t+1}(\mathbf{y}_{t+1}, \mathbf{x}_{t+1})\right\} \star \left\{\mathrm{D}_0^t(\mathbf{y}_t, \mathbf{x}_t) / \mathrm{D}_0^{t+1}(\mathbf{y}_t, \mathbf{x}_t)\right\}\right]^{\frac{1}{2}}$$

This decomposition is illustrated in Figure 3.2.

$$\text{Efficiency change} = \frac{Od / Of}{Oa / Ob}$$

$$\text{Technical change} = \{(Od/Oc)/(Od/Of)\} \star \{(Oa/Ob)/(Oa/Oe)\}^{1/2}$$

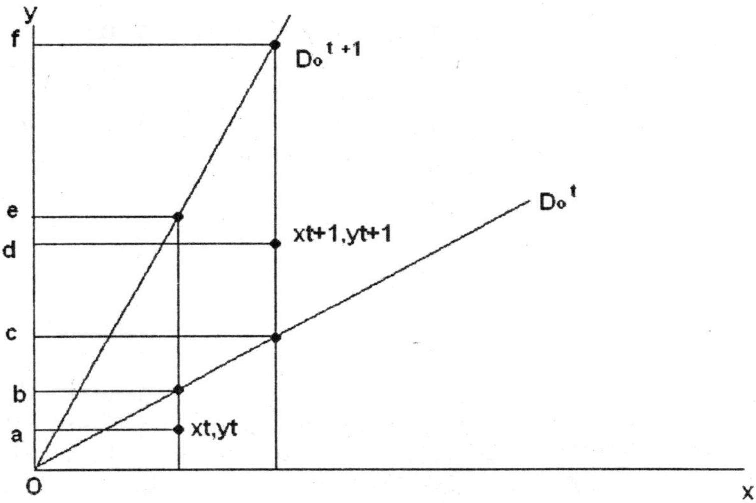

Figure 3.2: Illustration of Efficiency and Technical Change

Improvements yield Malmquist indexes with values greater than unity. Deterioration in performance over time is associated with a Malmquist index with a value less than unity.

The efficiency change and technical change components have the same interpretation.. Productivity growth may involve technical regress (if gains in efficiency being more than one, dominate the regress being less than one so that the product of the two is greater than one), or a fall in efficiency (if technical progress being more than one dominates the loss in efficiency being less than one so that the product of the two is greater than one). Similar possibilities hold for the case of decline in productivity.

3.3 Data Envelopment Analysis (DEA)

The Malmquist Productivity Index in terms of distance function is calculated using Tim Coelli's Data Envelopment Analysis Programme (DEAP) Version 2.1 (Coelli, 1996b). DEA is the non-parametric mathematical programming approach to frontier estimation. It involves the use of linear programming methods to construct a non-parametric piece-wise surface (or frontier) over the data, i.e., an envelopment frontier is constructed over the data points such that all observed points lie on or below the production frontier. For the simple case of an industry where one output is produced using two inputs, it can be visualized as a number of intersecting planes forming a tight fitting cover over a scatter of points in three dimensional space.

For an output oriented model, the linear programme assuming Constant Returns to Scale (CRS) technology is:

$$\max_{\phi,\lambda} \phi,$$

subject to
$$-\phi \mathbf{y}_{it} + Y_t \lambda \geq 0,$$
$$X_{i,t} - X_t \lambda > 0,$$
$$\lambda \geq 0,$$

where 1 ³ f ‹ ≤∮ and f – 1 is the proportional increase in outputs that could be achieved by the ith DMU (Decision Making Unit), with input quantities held constant. 1/f defines TE score (which varies between 0 and 1) and this is the TE score reported by DEAP. The DEA programming approach has a nice intuitive interpretation. Essentially, the problem takes the ith DMU and then seeks to radially expand the output vector y_i as much as possible while still remaining within the feasible output set. The boundary of this set is a piece-wise linear isoquant determined by the observed data points (i.e. all DMUs in the sample). The radial expansion of the output vector produces a projected point (X_1, Y_1) on the surface of this technology. This projected point is a linear combination of these observed data points.

The piece-wise linear form of the non-parametric frontier in DEA can cause difficulties if sections of piece-wise linear frontier run parallel to the axes. This is known as slack: in case of multiple inputs and/or multiple outputs both inputs and outputs slacks may appear. For ith DMU slacks will be equal to zero only if $Y\lambda - \phi Y_i = 0$ (output), and $X_i - X\lambda = 0$ (input) for given optimal values of ϕ and λ. The slacks are estimated using a multi-stage DEA in which a sequence of radial LPs is conducted to identify the efficient projected point. This projected point would lie on a line formed by joining points represented by some other efficient DMUs. These DMUs are usually referred to as peers of the inefficient DMU.

The CRS assumption is appropriate when all firms are operating at an optimal scale. A firm may not be operating at optimal scale due to imperfect competition, constraints on finance. Use of CRS specification when not all firms are operating at the optimal scale would result in measures of technical efficiency (TE) which are confounded by scale efficiencies (SE). The DEA model, therefore, needs to account for Variable Returns to Scale (VRS). The use of the VRS specification permits the calculation of technical efficiency devoid of these SE effects.

The CRS LP problem is modified to account for VRS by adding convexity constraints: $NI'\lambda = 1, \lambda \geq 0$ where NI is an N × 1 vector of ones. This approach forms a convex hull of intersecting planes which envelope the data points more tightly than the CRS conical hull and thus provides TE scores which are greater than or equal to those obtained using the CRS model. It may be noted that the convexity constraints ($NI'\lambda = 1$) essentially ensures that an inefficient firm is only "bench marked" against firms of similar size. That is the projected point (for that firm) on the DEA frontier will be a convex combination of observed firms. As this convexity restriction is not imposed in the CRS case, in a CRS DEA a firm may be bench marked against firms which are substantially larger (smaller) than it. In this instance the 'λ' weights will sum to a value greater than (less than) 1.

Technical Efficiency is estimated not only using the CRS model but also the VRS model. The scale efficiency (SE) is calculated using the relation $TE_{CRS} = TE_{VRS} \times SE$. The nature of scale inefficiency is determined by seeking whether NIRS (Non-Increasing Returns to Scale) TE score (obtained by using $NI' \leq 1$) is equal to VRS TE. If they are unequal than IRS exist for that DMU. When VRS option is specified, the DEAP programme conduct VRS, CRS and NIRS DEA and calculates scale efficiencies as well as technical efficiencies.

For a particular organisation, DEAP V 2.1 calculates four distance functions to measure the TFP change between two periods. This requires the solving of four linear programming (LP) problems.

We begin by assuming CRS technology

$$\left[d_0^t(\mathbf{x}_t, \mathbf{y}_t)\right]^{-1} = \max_{\phi,\lambda} \phi$$

Subject to

$$-\phi y_{it} + Y_t\lambda \geq 0,$$

$$X_{it} - X_t\lambda \geq 0,$$

$$\lambda \geq 0$$

The remaining three Linear Programming problems are simple variants of this:

$$(1)\ \left[d_0^{t+1}(x_{t+1}, y_{t+1})\right]^{-1} = \max_{\phi,\lambda} \phi,$$

$$\text{Subject to } -\phi y_{i,t+1} + Y_{t+1}\lambda \geq 0,$$

$$X_{i,t+1} - X_{t+1}\lambda \geq 0,$$

$$\lambda \geq 0$$

$$(2)\ [d_0^{t}(x_{t+1}, y_{t+1})]^{-1} = \max_{\phi,\lambda} \phi,$$

$$\text{Subject to } -\phi y_{i,t+1} + Y_t\lambda \geq 0,$$

$$X_{i,t+1} - X_t\lambda \geq 0,$$

$$\lambda \geq 0$$

$$(3)\ [d_o^{t+1}(x_t, y_t)]^{-1} = \max_{\phi,\lambda} \phi,$$

$$\text{Subject to } -\phi y_{it} + Y_{t+1}\lambda \geq 0,$$

$$X_{it} - X_{t+1}\lambda \geq 0,$$

$$\lambda \geq 0$$

One may interpret component output distance function measures as taking input quantities as given and seeking the greatest feasible proportional expansion of outputs given technology. No behavioural assumption concerning revenue maximization, cost minimization, or profit maximization is required. Nor is any information required with respect to input or output prices.

In the last two LP problems where production points are compared to technologies from different time periods, the ϕ parameter need not be ≥ 1, as it must be when calculating Farrell efficiencies. The point could lie above the feasible production set. This is most likely to occur in the LP where a production point from period $t+1$ is compared to technology in period t. If technical progress has occurred, then a value of $\phi < 1$ is possible. It could also possibly occur in the last LP if technical regress has occurred but this is less likely.

ϕ and λ's are likely to take different values in the above four LP's. The above four LP's must be calculated for each firm in the sample. Thus if there are 20 firms and 2 time periods one must calculate 80 LP's. As extra time periods are added, one must calculate an extra three LP's for each firm (to construct a chained index). If one has T time periods, one must calculate (3T-2) LP's for each firm in the sample. Hence, if one has N firms, one will need to calculate N*(3T-2) LP's. For example, with N = 20 firms and T = 10 time periods, this would provide 20*(3*10-2) = 560 LP's. The results on each and every firm for each and every adjacent pair of time periods can be tabulated, and/or summary measures across time and/or space can be presented.

The VRS/CRS option in the DEAP instruction file has no influence on the Malmquist DEA routine because both are used to calculate the various distances which are used to construct the Malmquist indices. The number of LP's calculated accordingly increases from N*(3T-2) to N*(4T-2) because the first two LPs given above have to be also calculated using the convexity restriction NI'λ= 1.

3.4 Stochastic Frontier Analysis (SFA)

A major shortcoming of the non-parametric frontier approach is that all deviations from the frontier such as measurement error and/or random shocks are assumed to be the result of technical inefficiency, thereby giving inflated estimates of technical inefficiency. The solution to this kind of 'noise' problem which has been widely accepted is the parametric stochastic frontier approach proposed by Aigner *et al.* (1977) and Meeusen and Broeck (1977). This involves the specification of a frontier function with an error term with two components: a symmetric error to account for noise and an asymmetric error to account for inefficiency. This approach has also been used for estimating technical efficiency.

Parametric estimation necessitates choosing a functional form for representing the production technology. But this is invariably subject to specification error. This has been overcome by choosing a flexible functional form which is also easy to calculate, and permits the imposition of the homogeneity condition. The translog functional form is specified for the distance function corresponding to a multi-output/multi-input technology with technical progress defined as a trend variable. (The Cobb-Douglas form is not an acceptable model because of its restrictive elasticity of substitution and scale properties).

The translog distance function for the case of M outputs and K inputs is specified as:

$$\ln D'_{0i} = \alpha_0 + \Sigma\alpha_m \ln y'_{mi} + 1/2\,\Sigma\Sigma\alpha_{mn} \ln y'_{mi} . \ln y'_{ni} + \Sigma\beta_k \ln + x'_{ki} +$$
$$\Sigma\Sigma\beta_{kl} \ln x'_{ki} \ln x'_{li} + \Sigma\Sigma\delta_{km} \ln x'_{ki} \ln y'_{mi} + \zeta t + \tfrac{1}{2}\zeta_{tt} t^2 +$$
$$\Sigma\nu_k \ln x'_{ki} t + \Sigma\phi_m \ln y'_{mi} t$$

where y's are the outputs, x's are the inputs and t is the trend variable in the model, and i = 1, 2, ...N represents the ith country and t = 1,2,....T. To obtain the frontier surface (i.e., the transformation function) one would set $D_{0i} = 1$, which implies the left hand side of the above equation is equal to zero.

The restrictions required for homogeneity of degree +1 in outputs are $\Sigma\alpha_m = 1$ and

$$\Sigma\alpha_{mn} = 0,\ m = 1, 2, \ldots\ldots, M, \text{ and } \Sigma\delta_{km=} 0,\ k = 1, 2, \ldots\ldots\ldots K,$$
$$\Sigma\phi_m = 0$$

and those required for symmetry are

$$\alpha_{mn} = \alpha_{nm},\ m, n = 1, 2, \ldots\ldots\ldots M, \text{ and } \beta_{kl} = \beta_{lk},\ k, l = 1, 2., ..k$$

The restrictions required for separability between inputs and outputs are $\delta_{km} = 0$, k= 1,2,...K, m = 1, 2, ... M.

For the purpose of estimation, we transform the translog function to an estimable form. Homogeneity implies that

$$D_0(x, \omega y) = \omega D_0(x, y), \text{ for any } \omega > 0$$

Hence, if we arbitrarily choose one of the outputs, such as the Mth output, and set $\omega = 1/y_M$ we obtain

$$D_o(x, y/y_M) = D_o(x, y)/y_M$$

Transforming into logs and rearranging the terms, the function can be rewritten with the output selected for normalization as the dependent variable as follows:

$\ln (D_{0i}/y_{Mi}) = TL(\mathbf{x}_i, \mathbf{y}_i/\mathbf{y}_{Mi}, t, \theta)$, i= 1, 2,.....N where θ is the set of parameters values.

or

$$\ln (D_{0i}) - \ln (\mathbf{y}_{Mi}) = TL(\mathbf{x}_i, \mathbf{y}_i/\mathbf{y}_{Mi}, t, \theta)$$

and hence

$$\ln (y_{Mi}) = TL(\mathbf{x}_i, \mathbf{y}_i / \mathbf{y}_{Mi}, t, \theta) - \ln (D_{0i})$$

What is required here is the selection of parameter values for the translog function which ensure the function fits the observed data as closely as possible while maintaining the requirement that $0 < D_{0i} \leq 1$, which implies that—infinity < $\ln (D_{0i}) \leq 0$. Setting $u = -\ln D_{0i}$ and adding a stochastic term we obtain a stochastic output distance function as:

$$-\ln (y_{Mi}) = TL(\mathbf{x}_i, \mathbf{y}_i / \mathbf{y}_{Mi}, t, \theta) + \varepsilon_{it}, \varepsilon_{it} = u_{it} + v_{it}$$

where ε is a composed error term allowing for inefficiency in production (*u*) and for noise (*v*). V_{it} s are random variables that take into account measurement errors and other random factors and the effects of explicative variables not considered by the model. They are independent variables and identically distributed with distribution N $(0, \sigma^2_v)$ and independent of the $U_{it}s$. Uit s are negative random variables associated with inefficiency. A half-normal distribution assumed by Aigner *et al.* (1977) has a mode at zero thereby implying high probability of inefficiency being in the neighbourhood of zero (thus relatively high technical efficiency). In practice, it may be possible to have a few efficient firms and many inefficient ones. Thus a truncated-normal distribution which is a generalization of the half-normal distribution is used. It is obtained by the truncation at zero of the normal distribution with mean μ and variance σ^2_u. These variables are assumed to be independent but not identically distributed and follow a normal distribution truncated at zero, N (μ_{it}, σ^2_u).

Moreover, as we are using panel data, technical inefficiency cannot be assumed to be time-invariant as T becomes large. This is because one would expect the managers to learn from previous experiences of the production process such that technical inefficiency effects would change in some persistent pattern over time. The technical inefficiency effects are assumed to be defined by:

$$u_{it} = \{ \exp [-\eta(t - T)]\} u_i,$$

where η is an unknown parameter to be estimated.

In this specification, if the ith country is observed in the last period of the panel, period T, then $u_{it} = u_i$ because the exponential function will have a value of one as $t = T$. Thus the random variable u_i can be considered as the technical inefficiency effect for the *i*[th] country in the last period of the panel. For earlier periods in the panel, the technical efficiency effects are the product of the technical inefficiency effect for the ith country at the last period of the panel and the value of the exponential function, exp $[-\eta(t-T)]$, whose value depends on the parameter η, and the number of periods before the last period of the panel—$(t-T) = T-t$. If the parameter η is positive then $u_{it} \geq u_i$ and conversely if η is less than 0 then $u_{it} \leq u_i$. In case of declining technical inefficiency effects, there would be a monotonic decrease in u_{it} towards the value at the last period of the panel. Further, the technical inefficiency effects of a different country at any given time period is equal to the same exponential function of the corresponding country specific inefficiency effect of the last period of the panel, thereby implying that the ordering of the countries according to the magnitude of technical inefficiency effects is the same for all periods. That is the time varying model of technical inefficiency chosen above does not account for situations in which some countries may be relatively inefficient initially but become relatively more efficient in subsequent periods.

Given appropriate distributional assumptions for *vi* and *ui*, the parameters of the stochastic distance function can be estimated. For the purpose of estimation, Tim Coelli's FRONTIER Version 4.1 can be used. The likelihood function has been parameterized in terms of $\sigma^2 = \sigma^2_u + \sigma^2_v$, $\gamma = \sigma^2_u / \sigma^2$. The parameters of the translog distance function are estimated simultaneously with four other parameters σ^2, γ, μ, and η using the maximum likelihood method. The procedure involved in estimating the parameters is to start with OLS estimators of the β, σ^2 followed by a grid search in which values of γ between 0 and 1 is given, and then in the final step the best estimates are taken as starting values for iterative maximization which obtains the ML estimates when the likelihood functions attains it global maximum. The predicted value of the distance for the *i*-th country $D_{0i} = \exp(-u_i)$ is not directly observable because u_i only appears as part of the composed error term. The predicted value of the output distance function for country *i* in period *t* can then be estimated as a conditional expectation:

$$D^t_{0i} = E\,[\exp(-u_{it}) \mid \varepsilon_{it}],$$

which is given directly by the FRONTIER Version 4.1.

3.5 Pricing

The methodology followed for pricing is to start with a critical examination of the existing procedure followed by India Post in costing and pricing of its products. Because of several shortcomings in the existing costing methodology, an outline of the method to be followed for attributing cost using Activity Based Costing has been indicated. The Universal Service Obligations for postal administrations is one unique feature, which needs to be incorporated into pricing decisions. Accordingly, the cost of Universal Service Obligation is also estimated, which may require to be factored into pricing decisions. The outcome of the results on productivity and efficiency has also been related to pricing decisions. Pricing decisions in the context of increasing competitions in the market is also examined. The costing and the pricing methodology in the context of India Post is discussed in detail in Chapter 5.

3.6 The Approach

This study on India Post begins with a global comparison of India Post with reference to 23 developing economies (including India), followed by comparison of India Post amongst the 11 developing economies of Asia.

Situation 1: Productivity of India Post is studied with reference to 23 countries.

Situation 2: Productivity of India Post is compared with reference to only the Asian countries taken from the above list of 23 countries.

Situation 3: The study also focused on the emerging economies.

There is a strong perception that there is a club of emerging and developing nations (China, India, Brazil, Russia, Indonesia, Mexico, and Turkey) which will outpace the lumbering G-7 (US, Japan, Germany, UK, France, Italy and Canada) on virtually every economic parameter by 2050. Post office as a means of communication and networking for the economy will also have an important role to play in the emerging economies. India Post being one of these emerging economies, productivity and efficiency of the emerging economies was also studied.

Situation 4: Also attempted in the study is the estimation of productivity and efficiency of the postal circles in India Post. For the purpose of our study only 19 postal circles have been taken. This is because three postal Circles, namely, Jharkhand, Chhattisgarh, and Uttarakhand were formed in the year January 2001 and as such the requisite data for these circles prior to 2001 are not available. For some outputs, as for example, savings bank, the data are still not available even after formation of the circles. Accordingly, the data for these three circles have been merged with their respective parent circles, i.e. with Bihar for Jharkhand, with M.P. for Chhattisgarh, and with U.P. for Uttarakhand.

Both non-parametric and parametric methods have been used for estimation. For the non-parametric estimation the DEA approach, Tim Coelli's DEAP Version 2.1 has been used. For the purpose of estimating technical efficiency both the CRS (Constant Returns to Scale) and the VRS (Variable Returns to Scale) assumptions have been made and the results on output, input and slacks have also been calculated. The stochastic frontier approach applying Tim Coelli's FRONTIER Version 4.1 has been used for parametric estimation.

Several hypotheses tests have been conducted to test the validity of the model. Also attempted in the study is to find out the factors affecting technical efficiency. For the ith country in the tth period the technical inefficiency effect u_{it} is obtained by truncation of N (μ, σ^2) distribution where, $\mu_{it} = Z_{it}\psi$ and Z is a vector of observable explanatory variables whose values are fixed constant and ψ is a vector of unknown parameters to be estimated.

It is assumed that there is no correlation amongst random errors and these variables, no heteroskedasticity in the random errors and the technical inefficiency effects. The above equation specifies that the means of the normal distributions which are truncated at zero to obtain the distributions of technical inefficiency effects are not the same but are functions of values of observable variables and a common vector of parameters. The ML estimation of this stochastic frontier model is also done using the FRONTIER 4.1 version.

An attempt is also made to link the productivity and efficiency results with pricing decisions of India Post. Ways and means of deciding prices of postal products for India Post in the present era of competition in the postal market is also discussed.

3.7 Data—Sources and Issues

Data have been taken from the Universal Postal Union site in case of international comparisons, and from Book of Information and other official publications in case of intra-national (Circle) comparisons. All the outputs have been included but for purpose of our study they have been put under broad categories. In case of study of the developing economies, the broad categories are as follows: (i) letter post items, both domestic as well as international; (ii) parcels, which include domestic and international ordinary, registered, and insured, and logistics; (iii) financial services such as number of money orders, domestic and international, and number of savings bank accounts, and (iv) registered and insured letters, domestic and international, second class mails including newspapers and advertisement mails. Because of differences in prices of outputs and to facilitate international comparisons, the outputs have been weighted by their percentage income contribution to the total income. Only two inputs: number of postal staff representing labour and number of post offices representing capital have been taken.

In the global and Asian comparison of the developing economies, data for the period 2001-2004 are used for the study as data on the percentage contribution of products to income were available for this period only. Those developing economies which had data on percentage contribution for at least three years out of the four years were shortlisted. Moreover, as delivery of postal objects to any addressee, to any destination (even when it is unprofitable to do so) still characterizes the universal service rendered by the majority of the PPOs (Public Postal Operators), the national territory's dimension and the population ought to be important considerations in selecting the countries. Thus, as India has a large area and very big population, therefore, in order to generate the same degree of geographical and institutional environment, countries in descending order of area and population were selected. Further, because India Post has a large number of post offices, all developing economies having less than 1,000 post offices were also excluded from the study.

The developing countries selected are the following:

Asia and Pacific: Bangladesh, China (People's Republic), India, Indonesia, Iran, Korea (People's Republic), Malaysia, Pakistan, Sri Lanka, Thailand, Vietnam.

Europe and CIS: Kazakhstan, Poland, Romania, Russian Federation, Turkey, Ukraine, Uzbekistan.

Latin American and Carribean: Argentina, Brazil, Mexico.

AFRICA: Egypt, Morocco.

In several cases, the data for a particular year were not available. Either the data of the previous year have been taken, or in case where the data of the first year were not available, then the data of the following year were taken. The only exception is that of Vietnam where the data of 2004 for letter post items have been taken for other three years also. Since Vietnam has more than 10,000 Post Offices, it was felt that Vietnam should be included in the study. Similarly, in respect of Brazil, figure for ordinary parcels for 2003 has been taken for 2001 and 2002. In respect of China, figure of 2002 for number of Savings Bank Account has been taken for 2001, 2003 and 2004.

Some economies which could not be included in the study for various reasons are the following:

(i) South Africa although having more than 1000 Post Offices was not included in the study because data for only 2001 were available in respect of some items such as Parcels.

(ii) Colombia and Nigeria though having more than 1000 Post Offices was excluded from the study because no data were available either for domestic money order or for savings bank.

(iii) Ghana had 1027 Post Offices in the first year, but the number of Post Offices came down below 1000 in the subsequent years. Moreover data for Money Orders were not available.

Data for 7 emerging economies have also been taken from the UPU site. As data for Russian Federation is available from 1991 onwards, the study uses the data for 15 years from the period 1991 to 2005. Incidentally, this was the time when the Indian economy also opened up and, coincidentally, even India Post started thinking in terms of computerization of its operations.

The following assumption regarding data was made while estimating the productivity and efficiency of the seven emerging economies.

Data of the previous year has been used in case of missing data. Certain exceptions are as follows:

Turkey: Data for 1996 in respect of number of full time staff have been used for the years 1991 to 1995.

Brazil: Data for 2000 in respect of Parcel have been used for the years, 2001, 2002.

China: The data for savings bank were available for only 4 years out of 15 years.

In order to have comparable figures, some bold assumptions were required to be made in respect of data on savings bank: data for 1991 were used for the years 1992 to 1994, while data for 1997 were used for the years 1998 to 2001 and data for 2002 were used for the years 2003 to 2005.

For postal circles of India Post, the data have been taken from the Book of Information published annually by the Department of Posts. Data for six years from 1999-2000 to 2004-2005 have been taken up for the study. Demands for Grants, Annual Reports, Book of Information, and other official documents have been used for studying the costing and pricing issues of India Post.

3.8 Summary

To sum up, the multiple-output multiple-input feature of India Post has been modelled using the distance function. Distance function has been used not only because its reciprocal gives Farrell measures of technical efficiency, but also because it is used to define the Malmquist Productivity Index which is very useful in calculating productivity growth in the presence of inefficiency. Another reason for using distance function is that it neither requires price or share data, nor behavioural assumption of cost-minimization, revenue-maximization, or profit-maximization. Different samples have been used for the study of productivity and efficiency of India Post, such as a sample of 23 developing economies, a sample of 11 Asian economies and a sample of 7 emerging economies. The productivity and efficiency at a disaggregated level, i.e. of the postal circles of India Post was also examined. Data have been taken from UPU site, Book of Information, and other official publications of India Post. Both non-parametric and parametric methods have been used for estimation. For the non-parametric estimation Tim Coelli's DEAP Version 2.1 has been used. The stochastic frontier approach applying Tim Coelli's FRONTIER Version 4.1 has been used for parametric estimation. Various tests of hypotheses have been done to test the validity of the model. The methodology followed for pricing is to start with a critical examination of the existing procedure followed by India Post in costing and pricing of its products. An outline of the method to be followed for attributing joint cost using Activity Based Costing has been indicated. Also estimated is the cost of Universal Service Obligation which may require to be factored into pricing decisions. The outcome of the results on productivity and efficiency has also been related to pricing decisions.

4

Productivity and Efficiency Analysis: Empirical Results

4.1 Introduction

Review of the studies on productivity and efficiency of postal administrations revealed that a comprehensive study on India Post is yet to be undertaken. It is also observed that any such study should be based on a consideration of multiple outputs and multiple inputs. Even given this consideration, some aggregation of products/services would be required because India Post handles a large number of products. Accordingly, in this study, all the postal products/services have been classified under broad categories taking care that none of the products/services in respect of which data are available have been omitted. The data have been taken from the Universal Postal Union site in case of international comparisons, and from the Book of Information and other official publications of the Department of Posts in case of intra-national comparisons. Both non-parametric (DEA) and parametric (SFA) methods have been used for estimation. However, in case of parametric estimation, only technical efficiencies have been estimated. For the non-parametric estimation Tim Coelli's DEAP Version 2.1 has been used. For the purpose of estimating technical efficiency both the CRS and the VRS assumptions have been made and the results on output, input and slacks have also been calculated. The stochastic frontier approach applying Tim Coelli's FRONTIER Version 4.1 has been used for parametric estimation. Various tests of hypotheses have also been done to test the validity of the model.

4.2 Global Comparison

For an international comparison of India Post with reference to other developing economies, 23 countries have been taken for study. There are 4 output variables and 2 input variables as defined below:

- y_1 is the letter post items weighted by percentage of income share linked to letter post items.
- y_2 is parcel weighted by percentage of income share linked to parcels and logistics.
- y_3 is financial services, i.e. money orders and savings bank accounts weighted by percentage of income share linked to postal financial services.
- y_4 is other products, i.e. second class mails and registered mails, etc. weighted by the percentage of income share linked to other products.

(Percentage of income linked to philately is small in case of most postal administrations. Also, in many cases the data were not available. Accordingly, the contribution of philately was ignored as it would not make much difference to the study).

- $\mathbf{X}_1$ is the number of equivalent workers in the PPO's (Public Postal Operators).

  (It was assumed that a part-time worker represents half of the contribution to production that a full-time worker makes. $\mathbf{X}_1$ is therefore taken as equal to the number of full-time officials plus half the number of part-time officials).
- $\mathbf{X}_2$ is the number of post offices which is applied as a proxy for capital stock investment following Maruyama and Nakajima (2002).

Tim Coelli's DEAP Version 2.1 has been used for the DEA. The performance of India Post for the four years is given in Table 4.1.

With the assumption of constant returns to scale, technical efficiency fell from 0.879 in year 2001 to 0.466 in year 2004. An efficiency change of 0.922 in 2004 does not say much on its own; in fact, efficiency stagnated at a low level, further falling from 0.505 in

Table 4.1: Technical Change, Efficiency Change and Total Factor Productivity of India Post 2001-2004

Year	*Technical Efficiency with Ref. to Technology in Year t-1*	*Technical Efficiency with Ref. to Technology in Year t*	*Technical Efficiency with Ref. to Technology in Year t+1*	*Efficiency Change*	*Technical Change*	*Total Factor Productivity Change*
2001	–	0.879	0.743	–	–	–
2002	0.887	0.750	0.539	0.854	1.182	1.010
2003	0.774	0.505	0.466	0.673	1.460	0.983
2004	0.505	0.466	–	0.922	1.085	1.000
Mean	–	–	–	0.809	1.233	0.998

the year 2003 to 0.466 in year 2004. Technical change which was 18 per cent in the year 2002, increased to 46 per cent in the year 2003, before falling to 8 per cent in the year 2004. The total factor productivity change remained stagnant with an average of 0.998.

The performance of India Post was also compared with some other major economies like China and Brazil. Both these countries showed a technical efficiency of 1.000 in each of the four years, i.e. they were on the production frontier throughout. However, the total factor productivity change in both these countries declined from 1.174 and 1.223 in the year 2002 to 0.969 and 0.925 in the year 2004 respectively. This fall was primarily due to decrease in the technical change in both the countries during the period 2002 to 2003, being 0.711 in case of China and 0.806 in case of Brazil. There were sharp increases in one of the inputs, namely, labour, in both the countries. In case of China, the weighted value of labour increased from 4.61 lakh to 5.27 lakh. This was not accompanied by requisite increase in outputs. The deflator required to bring the input-output of 2002 to the frontier technology of 2003 was almost double at 1.998. The same argument holds in case of Brazil also, though here the increase in labour was from 0.97 lakh to approximately 1.04 lakh, and the deflator required to bring the input-output of 2002 on to the frontier technology of 2003 was 1.351. The average efficiency change, technical change, and total factor productivity change of India Post with reference to other developing countries is given in Table 4.2.

The average total factor productivity change of all the countries for this period was 1.048, i.e., a growth of 4.8 per cent. The total factor productivity change of India Post stagnated at 0.998, whereas some of the countries which showed higher growth were Iran

Table 4.2: Malmquist Productivity Index—Summary of Country Means

Sl. No.	Countries	Efficiency Change	Technical Change	TFP Change
1.	Argentina	0.991	0.990	0.980
2.	Bangladesh	0.849	1.189	1.009
3.	Brazil	1.000	0.970	0.970
4.	China (People's Republic)	1.000	0.932	0.932
5.	Egypt	0.787	1.052	0.827
6.	India	0.809	1.233	0.998
7.	Indonesia	0.979	1.016	0.994
8.	Iran	1.480	1.183	1.752
9.	Kazakhstan	1.000	0.917	0.917
10.	Korea (People's Republic)	1.000	1.046	1.046
11.	Malaysia	1.000	1.091	1.091
12.	Mexico	0.975	0.988	0.963
13.	Morocco	1.011	1.119	1.131
14.	Pakistan	1.003	1.212	1.215
15.	Poland	1.000	1.049	1.049
16.	Romania	0.900	0.948	0.853
17.	Russian Federation	0.813	0.963	0.782
18.	Sri Lanka	0.961	0.999	0.960
19.	Thailand	1.000	0.991	0.991
20.	Turkey	1.036	1.038	1.076
21.	Ukraine	1.108	0.948	1.050
22.	Uzbekistan	2.179	0.949	2.068
23.	Vietnam	1.030	1.027	1.058
	Mean	1.014	1.033	1.048

(1.752), Korea (1.046), Malaysia (1.091), Pakistan (1.215), and Turkey (1.076). Iran with such huge growth in productivity deserves special mention. With efficiency as low as 0.408 in 2002, there was an increase in mail volume, both ordinary mails and registered mails, bringing Iran on the frontier with an efficiency of 1.000. This turn-around had the effect of giving an efficiency change of 2.451 and a total factor productivity of more than 3.0 in the year 2003, thereby raising the average total factor productivity to 1.752.

With the assumption of variable returns to scale, the technical efficiency of India Post which was 1.00 in the beginning years of the study declined to 0.90 in the penultimate year and ended up with 0.86 in the year 2004. Since the technical efficiency of India Post was less than 1.000, also calculated was the radial movement of the outputs and the inputs (including slacks) which could have enabled it to come on that portion of the production frontier where the input and output mixes would be as similar as possibly to that of the

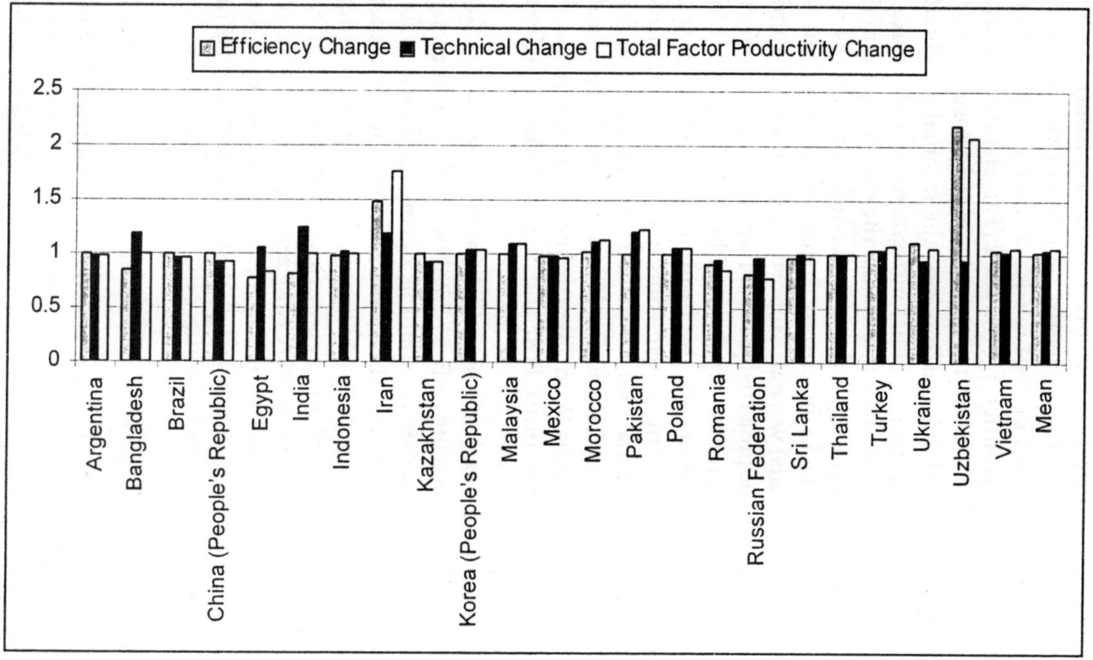

Figure 4.1: Technical Change, Efficiency Change and Total Factor Productivity of 23 Developing Countries

The figure is based on MPI given in Table 4.2.

Note: All Malmquist index averages are geometric means.

efficient points. A multi-stage DEA analysis for the year 2004 showed technical efficiency of 0.86, thereby implying that the outputs needed to be expanded by 1/0.86 to bring it on the frontier. The result shows that output 1, i.e., mails, which had the original weighted value of 174 crores in 2004 needed a radial movement of 27 crores to come on the frontier; for output 2 (Parcels) the original weighted value was 1.3 crores and required a radial movement of 0.22 crores; for output 3 (Financial Services) the original weighted value was 12.1 crores requiring a radial movement of 1.89 crores; and for output 4 (Registered and other mails) the original weighted value was 25.5 crores requiring a radial movement of 4 crores to come on the frontier. Slacks in output 2 (parcels) and output 4 (Registered and other mails) were also reported being 0.18 crore and 175 crores respectively. The projected point of India Post on the frontier lies on a line joining the points represented by Brazil, China, and Korea (Democratic Republic) on the frontier. This point on the frontier for India Post being linear combination of the points represented by Brazil, China, and Korea had weights of 0.108 for Brazil, 0.756 for China, and 0.136 for Korea. Brazil, China, and Korea were the peers of India Post. They define where the relevant part of the frontier is for India Post and hence define efficient production for India Post.

The results also showed an excess of 1,04,261 Post Offices for India Post (it should be having only 51,739 Post Offices in the year 2004). These surplus post offices would be having implications for pricing decisions. India Post was also found to be operating on that part of the production function which was showing decreasing returns to scale unlike several other countries which were found to be operating on the part showing increasing returns to scale: Mexico and Russia were on IRS, and Brazil, China, and Korea were on the CRS. It can be concluded from this study that India Post is a case of stagnation in productivity with surplus capacity and idle costs.

4.3 Asian Comparison

A comparative study of India Post with other Asian countries showed more or less similar results. With CRS assumption TE of India Post declined from 1.000 in 2001 to 0.75, 0.601, and 0.537 in the years 2002, 2003 and 2004. With VRS assumption, TE of India Post was found to be 1.000, except for the year 2003 when it was 0.906. It may be noted that the data for the year 2004 for India Post was assumed to be the same as that for the year 2003, as data for 2004 was not available on the UPU site. It therefore means that even with VRS assumption the TE of India Post declined from 1.00 to 0.906 in the year 2003.

The average efficiency change, technical change, and total factor productivity change of India Post with reference to other Asian countries is given in Table 4.3 :

Table 4.3: Malmquist Productivity Index—Summary of Country Means

Sl. No.	*Countries*	*Efficiency Change*	*Technical Change*	*Total Factor Productivity Change*
1.	Bangladesh	0.849	1.189	1.009
2.	China (People's Republic)	1.000	0.876	0.876
3.	India	0.813	1.201	0.976
4.	Indonesia	0.849	1.095	0.930
5.	Iran	1.480	1.169	1.731
6.	Korea (Rep.)	1.000	1.167	1.167
7.	Malaysia	1.000	1.086	1.086
8.	Pakistan	1.003	1.212	1.215
9.	Sri Lanka	0.961	1.060	1.019
10.	Thailand	1.000	0.986	0.986
11.	Vietnam	1.130	0.923	1.043
	Mean	0.995	1.082	1.076

As can be seen, total factor productivity of India Post showed a decline of 2.4 per cent, primarily because of the decline in efficiency. This could be attributed to a substantial fall in the mail volume and parcels traffic between the years 2001 to 2004: from 1400 crore to 900 crore in case of mails, and from 33 crore to 12.7 crore in case of parcels. On the other hand, one of the inputs, the number of post offices increased during this period, though labour did fall from 4.36 lakh to 4.14 lakh. However, technical change during this period was of the order of 20.1 per cent which compared very favourably with all other Asian countries.

Multi-stage DEA with VRS assumption for India Post for the year 2003 showed that India Post was on DRS portion of the production function. Output 1 (letter post items weighted in terms of income contribution) required a radial movement of 18.5 crore to enable India Post to come on the frontier; such radial movements for outputs 2, 3 and 4 were 0.14 crore, 1.23 crore, and 2.6 crore respectively. Outputs 2 and 4 also reported slack, being 0.13 crore

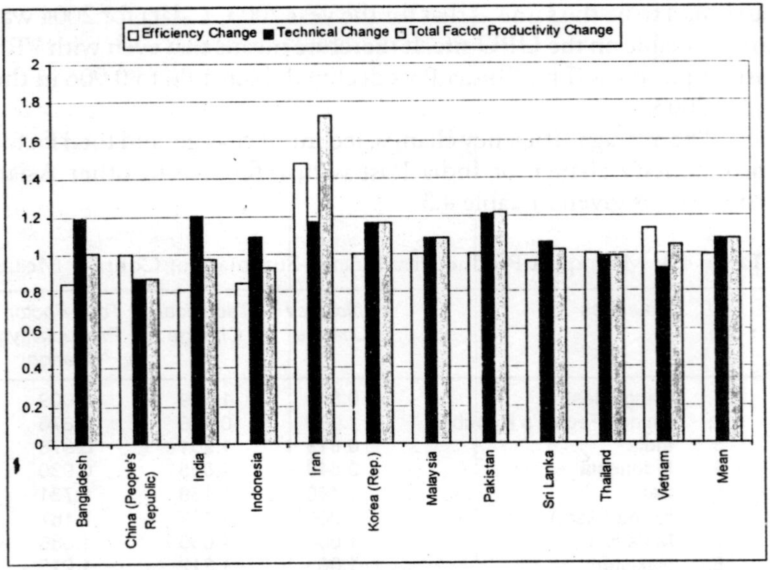

Figure 4.2: Technical Change, Efficiency Change and Total Factor Productivity of 11 Asian Countries

Note: The figure is based on MPI given in Table 4.3 .

for output 2 and 276.6 crore for output 4. India Post also showed a surplus of 1,05,509 Post Offices. Projection of India Post on the frontier was at a point formed by the line joining points represented by China, Iran and Korea with the weights being 0.772, 0.083 and 0.144 respectively. China and Korea continued to be relevant for India Post as found in global comparison, along with Iran (instead of Brazil found in global comparison). India Post needs to emulate the performance of these three postal administrations. The inevitable conclusion which emerges is that India Post showed a marginal decline in productivity with excess capacity and idle costs. This result is more or less similar to that obtained in the above global study of India Post with reference to 22 other countries with number of post offices found surplus being almost similar.

4.4 Emerging Economies

The technical efficiency of the group of emerging market economies

E7 (China, India, Brazil, Russia, Indonesia, Mexico and Turkey) was also estimated to see where India Post stood in this group. Three outputs and two inputs were considered for the study. The data pertained to the period 1991 to 2005.

- Y_1 is all kinds of mails, domestic and international, which included not only letter post items and second class mails but also included registered and insured mails.
- Y_2 is all kinds of parcels including registered and insured parcels, both domestic as well as international.
- Y_3 is all kinds of financial services in terms of numbers such as number of money orders, number of savings bank accounts.
- X_1 is the labour as defined above.
- X_2 is the number of Post Offices.

With CRS assumption and using DEA method, it is observed that Brazil showed technical efficiency of 1.00 in all 15 years, China in 9 out of 15 years and India in 7 out of 15 years. With VRS assumption the technical efficiency was found to be 1.000 for India Post except for the year 2003 when it was 0.977. Multi stage DEA analysis for the year 2003 for India Post revealed that India Post was on decreasing return to scale of the production function. Surplus inputs were also observed: 45532 surplus labour and 111565 excess Post Offices. This observation on surplus post offices is once again broadly in conformity with results found from our earlier studies (which also revealed excess post offices) on India Post.

Table 4.4: Malmquist Productivity Index—Summary of Country Means

Sl. No.	*Countries*	*Efficiency Change*	*Technical Change*	*Total Factor Productivity Change*
1.	Brazil	1.000	1.071	1.071
2.	China	1.036	0.977	1.012
3.	India	1.014	0.992	1.005
4.	Indonesia	1.067	0.967	1.032
5.	Mexico	1.009	1.025	1.035
6.	Russia	0.922	0.940	0.866
7.	Turkey	1.012	0.998	1.011
	Mean	1.008	0.995	1.002

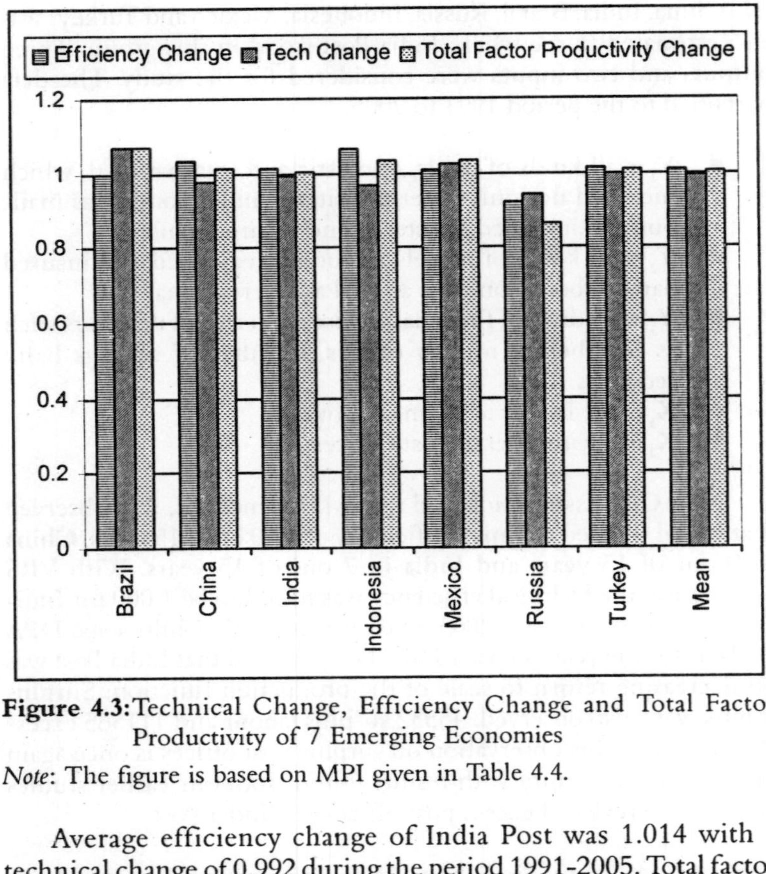

Figure 4.3: Technical Change, Efficiency Change and Total Factor Productivity of 7 Emerging Economies

Note: The figure is based on MPI given in Table 4.4.

Average efficiency change of India Post was 1.014 with a technical change of 0.992 during the period 1991-2005. Total factor productivity change of India Post in these 15 years was found to be 1.005. This is a growth of 0.5 per cent. On the other hand, Brazil showed a growth of 7.1 per cent with Total factor productivity change of 1.071, followed by Mexico with a growth of 3.5 per cent (TFP 1.035), and China and Turkey showing a growth of 1.2 and 1.1 per cent (TFP 1.012 and 1.011 respectively). Russia showed a decline in productivity to 0.866. Thus this study on emerging economies revealed that there was no growth in productivity in India Post over these 15 years, reinforcing the earlier findings on India Post with reference to the developing economies and Asian countries.

4.5 Efficiency Analysis Based on Stochastic Frontier Approach for Emerging Economies

Technical efficiency of these emerging economies was also estimated using the stochastic frontier approach. The translog distance function was specified in Chapter 3 and was used for estimation purposes. Tim Coelli's FRONTIER version 4.1 which uses maximum likelihood method was applied on the data for estimation.

The distance function was approximated by the translog functional form. For the purpose of estimation one of the outputs, namely, financial services, was selected as the dependent variable and as the variable of normalization for the other outputs.

Outputs: 'Y_1' (Mails) 'Y_2' (Parcels) 'Y_3' (Financial Services).
Inputs: 'X_1' (Labour), 'X_2' (No. of Post Offices).

The estimates of the parameters are given in Table 4.5.

Most of the maximum likelihood coefficients were accurately estimated and were significant as could be seen from *t* ratios. Technical inefficiency was correctly identified within the composed error term. The null hypothesis of no technical inefficiency effects in the model $\gamma = 0$ was rejected on applying the one sided generalized likelihood ratio test. Under regularity and under H_0, the large sample distribution of $-2\ln\lambda$ is χ^2, $[\lambda = L(H_0)/L(H_1)$, with degrees of freedom equal to the number of restrictions imposed (Greene, 2003). Under the null hypothesis: H_0: $\gamma = 0$ the value of the log likelihood function was –13.53 whereas under the alternative hypothesis the value of log likelihood function was 32.80. The test statistics was calculated as LR= $-2\ \{\ln[L(H_0)/L(H_1)]\} = -2\ (-13.53 - 32.80) = 92.66$ with number of restrictions = 3. This statistic has a mixed Chi-square distribution. It is observed that the one sided generalized likelihood ratio test of $\gamma = 0$ provided a statistic of 92.66 which was highly significant as it exceeded the 5 per cent critical value of 7.815 (χ^2_3). Hence the traditional average response function was not an adequate representation of the data. The share of technical inefficiency in total variance was 0.994, and the estimated standard error was 0.006. These results indicate that the vast majority of residual variation was due to the inefficiency effect. This is a slightly surprising result given the fact that there do occur error in measurement of the mail volume traffic of ordinary mails and therefore, one would normally expect data noise to play a larger role.

Table 4.5: Parametric Output Distance Function Estimation of Emerging Economies

	Variables		*Stochastic Model*	
			ML Estimates	*t Ratio*
	Intercept	α_0	–66.88	6.33
Outputs	ln y_1	α_1	5.538	3.31
	ln y_2	α_2	–5.275	4.23
	ln y_3	α_3	–1.263	
	ln y_1 Sq.	α_{11}	–0.593	4.37
	ln y_2 Sq.	α_{22}	–0.081	1.06
	ln y_3 Sq.	α_{33}	0.680	
	ln y_1 * ln y_2	α_{12}	0.677	3.65
	ln y_1 * ln y_3	α_{13}	–0.084	
	ln y_2 * ln y_3	α_{23}	–0.596	
Inputs	ln x_1	β_1	5.535	4.83
	ln x_2	β_2	5.703	4.09
	ln x_1 Sq.	β_{11}	–0.668	5.40
	ln x_2 Sq.	β_{22}	–0.648	3.85
	ln x_1 * ln x_2	β_{12}	0.567	2.34
Inputs Outputs	ln y_1 * ln x_1	δ_{11}	0.104	1.34
	ln y_2 * ln x_1	δ_{21}	–0.090	1.25
	ln y_3 * ln x_1	δ_{31}	–0.014	
	ln y_1 * ln x_2	δ_{12}	–0.375	3.70
	ln y_2 * ln x_2	δ_{22}	0.405	4.38
	ln y_3 * ln x_2	δ_{32}	–0.030	
Technical Change	t	ζ	0.776	5.37
	t Sq.	ζ_{11}	0.001	0.40
	ln x_1 * t	ν_1	–0.075	6.02
	ln x_2 * t	ν_2	0.026	1.64
	ln y_1 * t	ϕ_1	–0.041	3.26
	ln y_2 * t	ϕ_2	0.033	4.29
	ln y_3 * t	ϕ_3	0.008	
Other ML parameters	σ^2		4.023	1,09
	γ		0.994	168.15
	μ		–4.003	0.74
	η		–0.0998	6.10

Notes: (1) Underlined parameters are calculated by applying homogeneity conditions. (2) All the parameters are multiplied by –1.

Several other hypotheses were postulated to see whether our model adequately represented the data.

(i) $H_0: \mu = \eta = 0$ The value of μ was not found to be significant although that of η was significant. In order to see whether the truncated normal distribution was not an adequate representation of the error component, a composite null hypothesis of both $\mu = \eta = 0$ was also tested to see whether the model had time-invariant inefficiency effects with half normal distribution. The value of the log likelihood function was 17.38. Hence the value of the generalized likelihood ratio statistics for testing the null hypothesis was calculated as: LR = –2 (17.38–32.80) = 30.84. This value was compared with the upper 5 per cent point for χ^2 with two restrictions which was 5.99. Thus the hypothesis that the model had time invariant inefficiency effects with half normal distribution was rejected.

(ii) $H_0: \zeta = \zeta_{tt} = \nu_1 = \nu_2 = \phi_1 = \phi_2 = \phi_3 = 0$
When focused on technical change it was observed that most of the parameters associated with the trend variables were significant. To further substantiate this the model was estimated without the trend variable so as to test the hypothesis that there was no effect of trend variables (Negative parameters indicate positive changes in the technology. A positive parameter indicates technical regression. It was found that the value of t was positive and accordingly it was indicative of technical regression). The log likelihood value was –11.63. The likelihood ratio test was therefore –2 (–11.63 –32.80) = 88.86. (LR χ^2 = 12.59 with 6 degrees of freedom and 5 per cent level of significance). Thus, LR test on these parameters allowed to reject the null hypothesis of no technical change.

(iii) $H_0: \eta = 0$: A special case of the time-varying inefficiency model is the time-invariant model, which arises when $\eta = 0$. Accordingly, the model was estimated assuming $\eta = 0$. The log likelihood function was found to be 17.60. The generalized LR statistic for testing for absence of time-varying technical inefficiency effects from the frontier was calculated to be LR = –2 (17.60 – 32.80) = 30.40. This value was significant because it exceeded the critical value of $\chi^2_1 = 3.84$ at 5 per cent level of significance. Thus the null hypothesis of no change in technical inefficiency effects over time was rejected.

(iv) $H_0: \alpha_{11}=\alpha_{22}=\alpha_{12}=\beta_{11}=\beta_{22}=\beta_{12}=\delta_{11}=\delta_{21}=\delta_{12}=\delta_{22}=\zeta_{\tau\tau}=\nu_1 = \nu_2=\phi_1=\phi_2=0$

The second order output cross product term α_{12} had the correct sign (+) so as to encourage the transformation curve to have a concave shape rather than the convex Cobb-Douglas shape that would result if this term was 0. In fact a further hypothesis of interest was to see whether the Cobb-Douglas function was an adequate representation of the data given the specifications of the translog model. To test the null hypothesis that the second order coefficients of the translog frontier were simultaneously zero, the data set for the Cobb-Douglas model was created and the function estimated. The output file for estimating this Cobb-Douglas model using frontier gave the value of log likelihood function as –43.85. Hence the value of the generalized likelihood ratio test for testing the null hypothesis of a Cobb-Douglas model was calculated as:

$$LR = -2\,(-43.85-32.80) = 153.30$$

This value was compared with the upper 5 per cent point for the χ^2_{15} distribution which was 24.996. Thus the null hypothesis that the Cobb-Douglas frontier was an adequate representation of the data was rejected given the specifications of the translog frontier.

In terms of technical efficiency, India Post was ranked fourth amongst these seven emerging economies in the following order: Russia, Turkey, Indonesia, India, Brazil, Mexico, and China. Given the nature of the technical inefficiency model used in the study, the order of ranking according to the magnitude of the technical inefficiency effects would be preserved at all time periods of the sample. This is because the technical inefficiency effects of different countries at any given time period, *t*, are equal to same exponential function, exp $[-\eta(t-T)]$ of the corresponding country-specific inefficiency effects at the last period of the panel. The value of η in the study was negative, which meant that $u_{it} < u_i$, i.e., the technical efficiency should be declining proportionately as we go further from the last period of the panel. But in our case the technical efficiency is E[exp($-u_{it}$)] and thus the technical efficiency should be increasing as we go further away from the last period of the panel. The mean technical efficiency in the first year 1991 was 0.84, whereas in the last year 2005 it was 0.58. In case of India Post the technical efficiency was 0.85 in 1991 whereas it was 0.53 in the year 2005. The technical efficiencies of the seven postal administrations for the year 1991 and 2005 are given in Table 4.6 :

Table 4.6: Technical Efficiency of 7 Emerging Economies

Country	*Technical Efficiency*	
	1991	*2005*
Brazil	0.78	0.37
China	0.58	0.11
India	0.85	0.53
Indonesia	0.97	0.89
Mexico	0.77	0.36
Russia	0.98	0.92
Turkey	0.97	0.90

A technical efficiency model was also estimated with two regressors for explaining the technical efficiency, namely, population per PO as Z_1 and mails per capita as Z_2. The log likelihood ratio with number of restrictions 4 was 430.32 thus indicating the acceptability of the hypothesis that there was technical inefficiency in the sample. The value of Gamma was found to be 0.999 (with a very high *t* ratio). Both the regressors, namely population per post office and mails per capita were found significant. The value of Z_1 was 0.99 (*t* ratio 41.28) and that of Z_2 was 0.93 (*t* ratio 40.34). Thus the results showed that both population per Post Office and mails per capita affect technical efficiency. The mean efficiency of the sample was found to be 0.42 but the efficiency of India Post in each of the years was higher than this mean efficiency.

4.6 Efficiency Analysis Based on Stochastic Frontier Approach for Postal Circles

The productivity and efficiency of India Post at the level of the Postal Circles, i.e. at a certain level of disaggregation was also examined.

- Y_1 is ordinary mails but excludes registered and insured mails.

- Y_2 is registered mails which also includes all kinds of parcels and insurance service.
- Y_3 is financial services as defined above.
- X_1 is labour as defined above.
- X_2 is number of post offices.

The only difference in the definition of output relates to Y_1 and Y_2. In the study on emerging economies, Y_1 included all kinds of mails including registered mails, and Y_2 included parcels. In this study of Postal Circles in India, Y_1 includes only ordinary mails, and Y_2 is registered mails including parcels.

The stochastic frontier approach was used for estimating technical efficiency. The likelihood ratio test was found to be significant (LR test with three restrictions 82.79). Thus, the hypothesis that there was technical inefficiency prevailing in the circles could not be rejected. The value of γ was found to be 0.84 with *t* ratio 24.84. The mean technical efficiency of the circles was 0.697, with a mean efficiency of 0.70 in the first year which because of negative value of η consistently declined to a value of 0.69 in the last year.

The values of the estimated parameters are given in Table 4.7.

Most of the parameters were found to be significant. However, *t*, the trend variable, and η, the change in technical efficiency were not significant thereby implying that from 1999 to 2004 there was neither technical progress nor change in technical efficiency. Another estimation was therefore undertaken where the effect of the time trend as well as unchanging technical efficiency was modeled to be zero, i.e. $\zeta = \zeta_{\tau\tau} = \nu_1 = \nu_2 = \phi_1 = \phi_2 = \eta = 0$. The value of the log likelihood function comes to 103.57. The value of log likelihood function in the earlier case was 112.40. Thus, LR= –2 {ln[L(Ho)/L(H1)]}= –2 (103.57 – 112.40) = 17.66. The value of χ^2 with seven degrees of freedom at 5 per cent level of significance is 14.067. Thus, the hypothesis that the trend variables as well as the value of the η being 0 could not be accepted. It therefore implied that technical change which was modeled by using the time trend is valid, as also the assertion that the technical efficiency was undergoing change during the six year period.

The validity of the translog function as representative of the model was tested with reference to the Cobb-Douglas model, i.e.

$$\alpha_{11} = \alpha_{22} = \alpha_{12} = \beta_{11} = \beta_{22} = \beta_{12} = \delta_{11} = \delta_{21} = \delta_{12} = \delta_{22} = \zeta_{tt} = \nu_1 = \nu_2 = \phi_1 = \phi_2 = 0$$

Table 4.7: Parametric Output Distance Function Estimations of Postal Circles

	Variables		*Stochastic Model*	
			ML Estimates	*t Ratio*
	Intercept	α_0	5.97	6.02
Outputs	ln y_1	α_1	–0.81	0.99
	ln y_2	α_2	–0.84	1.27
	ln y_3	α_3	0.65	
	ln y_1 Sq.	α_{11}	0.03	0.31
	ln y_2 Sq.	α_{22}	–0.45	5.17
	ln y_3 Sq.	α_{33}	0.24	
	ln y_1 * ln y_2	α_{12}	0.33	3.13
	ln y_1 * ln y_3	α_{13}	–0.36	
	ln y_2 * ln y_3	α_{23}	0.12	
Inputs	ln x_1	β_1	2.52	3.68
	ln x_2	β_2	–1.27	1.69
	ln x_1 Sq.	β_{11}	–0.76	3.39
	ln x_2 Sq.	β_{22}	–0.68	3.57
	ln x_1 * ln x_2	β_{12}	1.40	3.64
Inputs Outputs	ln y_1 * ln x_1	δ_{11}	0.02	0.18
	ln y_2 * ln x_1	δ_{21}	0.44	3.90
	ln y_3 * ln x_1	δ_{31}	–0.46	
	ln y_1 * ln x_2	δ_{12}	0.02	0.14
	ln y_2 * ln x_2	δ_{22}	–0.51	4.34
	ln y_3 * ln x_2	δ_{32}	*0.49*	
Technical Change	T	ζ	0.07	0.56
	t Sq.	ζ_{tt}	0.006	0.75
	ln x_1 * t	v_1	0.02	0.82
	ln x_2 * t	v_2	–0.03	1.46
	ln y_1 * t	ϕ_1	–0.007	0.36
	ln y_2 * t	ϕ_2	0.012	0.75
	ln y_3 * t	ϕ_3	*–0.005*	
Other ML parameters	σ^2		0.028	5.53
	γ		0.845	24.84
	μ		0.309	3.90
	η		–0.011	0.46

Note: (1) Underlined parameters are calculated by applying homogeneity conditions. (2) All the parameters are multiplied by –1.

The value of log likelihood function was 93.30

$$LR = -2\ \{\ln[L(H_0)/L(H_1)]\}$$
$$= -2\ (93.30 - 112.40) = 38.20$$

The value of χ^2 with fifteen degrees of freedom at 5 per cent level of significance was 24.99. Thus, the hypothesis that the model could be represented by Cobb-Douglas function was rejected. Accordingly, the representation of the function by translog was appropriate.

4.7 Efficiency Analysis of Postal Circles Based on DEA

Non-parametric estimation using DEAP 2.1 version with CRS showed a decline in the mean technical efficiency of Postal Circles from 0.758 in the year 1999 to 0.662 in the year 2004. Delhi, Haryana, and Kerala Postal Circles showed technical efficiency of 1.00, West Bengal improved its efficiency from 0.92 in 1999 to 1.00 in 2004. The other postal circles showed fluctuating technical efficiency during this period ending up with a decline in efficiency except that of Punjab Postal Circle.

With the assumption of variables returns to scale (VRS) this decline in the mean technical efficiency of the Circles was from 0.845 to 0.798 during this period. Apart from Delhi, Haryana, and Kerala, four more postal circles, namely J&K, Maharashtra, Tamil Nadu, and West Bengal Circles also showed technical efficiency of 1.000. Gujarat, Andhra Pradesh, and North East which were on the frontier in some of the earlier years ended up with a TE of 0.70, 0.815, and 0.77 respectively in the year 2004. Karnataka and U.P. were the two postal circles which showed an increase in TE from 0.88 to 0.93 during this period (Punjab postal circle showed an increase from 0.65 to 0.78).

In order to assess excess capacity in outputs, and surplus inputs, a multi stage DEA assuming VRS was applied on the data for the year 2004. The radial movement in output depicts the increase in output required to bring the circles on to the production frontier.

A large number of surplus post offices were also observed in most of the postal circles (42142 post offices). For example, Andhra Pradesh showed a surplus of 5560 post offices, Bihar 5050 surplus post offices, Gujarat 2335 surplus post offices, Karnataka 2765

Table 4.8: Projected Outputs of Postal Circles

Sl. No.	Circles	Figure in Crores (Slacks Shown in Brackets)								
		Original Value			Radial Movement/(Slacks)			Projected Value		
		Output 1	Output 2	Output 3	Output 1	Output 2	Output 3	Output 1	Output 2	Output 3
1.	Andhra Pradesh	72	12	15	16	3 (8)	3.5 (2.1)	88	23	20.6
2.	Assam	28.3	0.22	0.47	8.2	0.06 (0.36)	0.14 (.08)	36.5	0.64	0.69
3.	Bihar	28	0.8	1.2	27	0.78	1.2	55	1.58	2.4
4.	Delhi	19.7	1.3	0.64	–	–	–	19.7	1.3	0.64
5.	Gujarat	57	1.17	1.42	23	0.46	0.56	80	1.63	1.98
6.	Haryana	7.9	0.31	1.5	–	–	–	7.9	0.31	1.5
7.	Himachal Pradesh	6.2	0.18	0.37	6.4	0.19	0.37	12.6	0.37	0.74
8.	Jammu and Kashmir	04	0.12	0.25	–	–	–	4	0.12	0.25
9.	Karnataka	35.7	0.92	2.48	2.7	0.7 (0.49)	0.19	38.4	1.48	2.67
10.	Kerala	85	1.4	1.3	–	–	–	85	1.4	1.3
11.	Madhya Pradesh	26	0.67	0.65	48	1.23	1.19 (0.03)	74	1.90	1.87
12.	Maharashtra	90	2.7	2.4	–	–	–	90	2.7	2.4
13.	North East	14.5	0.24	0.35	5.4	0.09 (.04)	0.13	19.9	.37	0.48
14.	Orissa	19.6	0.78	0.71	19.2	0.77	0.7	38.8	1.55	1.41
15.	Punjab	22.2	0.73	0.69	5.3	0.18	0.17	27.5	0.91	0.86
16.	Rajasthan	21	0.66	1.33	12	0.39	0.79	33	1.05	2.12
17.	Tamil Nadu	81	1.8	3.7	–	–	–	81	1.8	3.7
18.	Uttar Pradesh	58.3	2.46	3.4	4.4	0.18	0.25	62.7	2.64	3.65
19.	West Bengal	37	3.6	3.7	–	–	–	37	3.6	3.7

post offices, Madhya Pradesh 5035 surplus post offices, Orissa 4411 surplus post offices, Rajasthan 4423 surplus post offices, Uttar Pradesh 9218 surplus post offices (Uttar Pradesh circle also showed an excess manpower of 9022). Surplus post offices were also found as observed earlier, thus further confirming our findings.

The projected points of the circles on the frontier were linear combination of the points represented by the efficient circles. Karnataka could come on the frontier at a point which would be a linear combination of the points represented by West Bengal, Tamil Nadu and Haryana; thus Karnataka should look up to these peer circles for improving its performance. In case of Madhya Pradesh the circles which should be looked at are Kerala, West Bengal and Maharashtra; that for Uttar Pradesh would be West Bengal, Maharashtra and Tamil Nadu. The peer circles for each circle are given in Table 4.9.

Table 4.9: Peers of Postal Circles

Sl.No.	*Circles*	*Peer Circles*			
1.	Andhra Pradesh	Kerala	Maharashtra		
2.	Assam	Kerala	J&K		
3.	Bihar	Kerala	West Bengal	Tamil Nadu	Haryana
4.	Delhi	Delhi			
5.	Gujarat	Kerala	Haryana	Tamil Nadu	West Bengal
6.	Haryana	Haryana			
7.	Himachal Pradesh	Kerala	Haryana	Delhi	J&K
8.	Jammu and Kashmir	J&K			
9.	Karnataka	West Bengal	Haryana	Tamil Nadu	
10.	Kerala	Kerala			
11.	Madhya Pradesh	Kerala	West Bengal	Maharashtra	
12.	Maharashtra	Maharashtra			
13.	North East	Kerala	Haryana	J&K	
14.	Orissa	Kerala	West Bengal	Delhi	Haryana
15.	Punjab	Kerala	Haryana	Delhi	J&K
16.	Rajasthan	West Bengal	Tamil Nadu	Kerala	Haryana
17.	Tamil Nadu	Tamil Nadu			
18.	Uttar Pradesh	West Bengal	Tamil Nadu	Maharashtra	
19.	West Bengal	West Bengal			

It could be seen that Kerala needed to be emulated by 10 circles, followed by Haryana which should be emulated by 8 circles, and West Bengal by 7 circles. Smaller circles such as Assam, Himachal Pradesh, J&K, North Eastern Circle and Punjab postal circles were found operating on the increasing returns to scale (IRS) portion of the production function. Other postal circles were on the decreasing returns to scale (DRS), except for the four postal circles, namely Delhi, Haryana, Kerala and West Bengal, which were on the frontier with TE of 1.000.

The average efficiency change, technical change, and total factor productivity change of the circles during this period was also analysed to see whether the average productivity change for India Post conformed to the results obtained in the global and Asian context. The figures are given in Table 4.10.

Table 4.10: Malmquist Productivity Index—Summary of Circle Means

Sl. No.	*Circles*	*Efficiency Change*	*Technical Change*	*Total Factor Productivity Change*
1.	Andhra Pradesh	0.882	0.976	0.861
2.	Assam	0.972	0.978	0.951
3.	Bihar	0.959	1.048	1.004
4.	Delhi	1.000	0.935	0.935
5.	Gujarat	0.914	0.994	0.908
6.	Haryana	1.000	1.075	1.075
7.	Himachal Pradesh	0.957	1.032	0.988
8.	Jammu and Kashmir	0.972	1.045	1.016
9.	Karnataka	0.960	1.011	0.971
10.	Kerala	1.000	0.980	0.980
11.	Madhya Pradesh	0.939	0.975	0.916
12.	Maharashtra	0.954	0.984	0.938
13.	North East	0.986	0.985	0.971
14.	Orissa	0.996	0.974	0.971
15.	Punjab	1.032	0.980	1.011
16.	Rajasthan	0.978	1.026	1.004
17.	Tamil Nadu	0.950	1.021	0.970
18.	Uttasr Pradesh	0.978	1.005	0.983
19.	West Bengal	1.015	1.019	1.035
	Mean	0.970	1.002	0.972

From the above table, it is seen that except for Haryana and West Bengal circles which showed a total factor productivity change of 7.5 per cent and 3.5 per cent respectively, other circles are either showing stagnation or decline in productivity. The average total factor productivity of the circles for these 6 years was 0.972. The study of the postal circles over this period also confirms the conclusion already derived earlier that India Post is a case of stagnation/marginal decline in productivity.

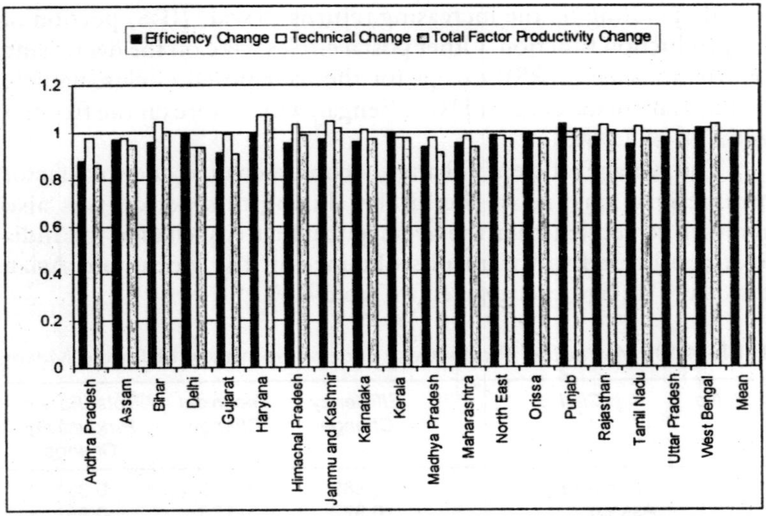

Figure 4.4: Technical Change, Efficiency Change and Total Factor Productivity of Postal Circles in India

Note: The figure is based on MPI given in Table 4.10.

4.8 Summary

The study shows that irrespective of the samples used, the empirical findings are the same regarding productivity of India Post. It is either stagnating, or showing a marginal decline in productivity, accompanied by surplus capacity in inputs. This is not a very surprising result given the fact that fall in outputs have not been accompanied by concomitant decline in inputs: mail volume traffic fell from 1550 crore in 1999 to 714 crore in 2005; labour from 6.01 lakh to 5.37 lakh. Though financial services transactions showed an increase from 25 crore to 28 crore, the number of post offices also increased marginally from 1.54 lakh to 1.55 lakh. Significantly, some of the other emerging economies especially Brazil and China showed increase in outputs handled by them. The study at the disaggregated level, i.e. of the postal circles over this period also confirms this conclusion that India Post is a case of stagnation/ marginal decline in productivity.

5

Pricing in India Post

5.1 Introduction

Postal pricing practices in all countries to a greater or lesser extent are inefficient. This inefficiency arises either within mail categories (e.g. the uniform price) and/or between categories (e.g. loss making activities being supported by profits from other categories). However, postal rate making has been moving towards greater efficiency in recent years, specially as postal operations have either been taken out of government departments and are being corporatized and subject to competition and/or disentangled from telecommunications operations. With corporatization have come the requirements to recover costs, a more profit—like incentive structure and more independence in the pricing of products.

Current pricing practices of postal services in most countries are based on broad guidelines which are as follows:

(i) Prices should be competitive and should be so designed that they improve the productivity and efficiency of the organization.
(ii) A reasonable tariff for a basic service to improve universal obligations.
(iii) Prices should at least be equal to the variable cost of the product.
(iv) Financial self-sufficiency of post office.

Pricing decisions require an accurate assessment of costs of products. The entire expenditure of India Post is allocated on each product/service. Revision in prices, for some of the products, for example premium products such as speed post is decided by the Government whereas in the case of others such as traditional products like postcards, etc. (i.e. those listed in First Schedule of the Indian Post Office Act) it is decided by the Parliament. A comprehensive examination of the present system of costing of products/services followed by India Post is attempted. This is required as costs provide a useful preliminary basis for pricing of products/services.

5.2 Current Costing Methodology

Since 1970, India Post has been following a cost accounting methodology which has been useful to ascertain the cost of different products/services based on figures which are taken from the Demands for Grants of the Department of Posts, which is part of the Annual Budget of the Government of India. The costing exercise for any year commences only after the actual expenditure for the year is available and the enumerated assessed traffic exercise is completed. Projected estimates of average costs of services for the current year is also prepared simultaneously for which Budget Estimates (BE) are available, by raising the actual cost by an escalation factor (BE of Expenditure/Actual Expenditure).

The main stages in the costing system are:

(a) Classification of total expenditure for costing purposes into various functions/services rendered by India Post,
(b) Determination of the output, i.e. the traffic of product/service, like the number of post cards, inland letters, etc. handled in a year, and
(c) Arriving at the cost per unit of service and comparing the same with the average revenue to determine surplus or deficit position.

Actual expenditure taken from the Demands for Grants is classified first into different cost categories in terms of operations, and expenses are then allocated on the products/services. The different operations are given below.

Post Office (PO) Operations

Expenses taken from Demands for Grants are allocated amongst clerical (Class-III) handling, Group 'D' assistance, delivery charges and collection charges on the basis of ratio of the product of average pay and the number of employees in each category to the sum total of product of average pay and number of employees of all categories. The allocation is illustrated as follows:

- Let X be total expenses on PO operations.
- Let w_{ij} be the average emolument for a particular category and l_{ij} be the number of employees in that category.
  where
    i= 1, 2, 3, 4 represents Clerical (Class-III) handling, Group 'D' assistance, delivery charges and collection charges respectively,
    j= 1 for dept employee, and 2 for part time employee (extra departmental employee)

  Then, X_{1j} (share of X in class III handling)

  $$= (w_{1j}\, l_{1j} / \Sigma_i \Sigma_j w_{ij} l_{ij}) \star X$$

  and similarly for $X_{2j}, X_{3j}, X_{4j}, j = 1, 2$
  where $\Sigma_i \Sigma_j X_{ij} = X$

In this way, share of clerical handling, etc., can be calculated, which for a particular year was projected to be 61.48 per cent for clerical handling, while for group D assistance it was projected to be 14.42 per cent, for delivery charges 22.45 per cent and for collection charges 1.65 per cent. From the share of class III handling, a predetermined percentage allocation is made for back office operations like cash handling, accounts, administration, etc., in respect of products such as registered articles, parcels, money orders, savings bank operations, etc. X_{ij} is allocated amongst the products/services primarily on the basis of ratio arrived at by multiplying the traffic and time factor taken for performing the service to the sum total of all the products multiplied by their respective time factors. For a particular year, in case of one product, namely, unregistered mail, the product of traffic and time factor was 8397 lakh of minutes. The total traffic of all the products multiplied by their respective time factor was 94842 lakh of minutes.

The allocation of cost of class III handling on this product would be equal to (8397/94842) multiplied by the expenses on post office operations for class III handling.

Railway Mail Service (RMS) Charges

The expenses taken from Demands for Grants are distributed amongst the products as follows:

(a) Let n_i = Traffic figure *time factor for handling product i

$$i = 1, 2, \ldots\ldots\ldots\ldots n$$

Total time factor = Σn_i

Allocation of RMS charges on a particular product = $(n_i/\Sigma n_i)$* total expenses on RMS operations.

Transport (Conveyance) Operations

The expenses on foreign mails are first deducted from the expenses on air freight charges. The allocation on the products/services is as follows:

Let w_i = (Average weight of a product) * (traffic), with total weight being Σw_i.

Allocation of expenses on the product i = $(w_i/\Sigma w_i)$* (total expenses on transport charges by air).

The same procedure is followed in respect of surface transport charges.

Note:

1. Average weight of product is determined by a sample survey covering three HPOs in each Circle.
2. The charge does not reflect distance or cost of transportation in the area.

Manufacturing (of Postal Stamps and Stationery) Operations

The actual cost of printing of stamp is distributed to all relevant services on the basis of ratio determined by multiplying the traffic of each product with their respective average revenues to the sum total of all products multiplied by their respective revenues.

Printing and Stationery Operations

The expenditure is first distributed in following three categories as per pre-determined fixed ratios:

1.	General Forms	17 per cent
2.	Ordinary Mail	42 per cent
3.	Other Forms	41 per cent

The expenditure arrived as above is further apportioned among the products/services on the basis of traffic.

Post Office Supervision Operations

The Post Office supervision expenses are distributed to all the services on the basis of percentage of Post Office operation expenses.

Other Overhead Expenses

Other overhead expenses, i.e. Accommodation, Administration, Accounts and Audit are distributed on the basis of ratio of total expenses of Post Office operation + RMS charges + Post Office supervision.

The cost of each of the product/service calculated by the above method is then taken as a basis for proposing revision in prices of the products/services. For example, for the year 2003-04, the cost of one product, namely, parcel, was calculated as Rs. 80.94 against average revenue of Rs. 57.17. A proposal for revising tariff of this product could be part of the Budget Estimates for the year 2004-05, which if it would have been accepted by the Government would have formed part of the Central Budget.

It is seen thus that traffic and a standard time factor for handling the products are two important ingredients in deciding the cost (or price) of the products/services. But the data on traffic is not adequately reliable for mail products/services. In case of mails, India Post classifies traffic as recorded mails and unrecorded (or unaccounted mails). Accurate quantitative details of recorded mails are available but the same cannot be said of unaccounted mails. The basis for working out the quantity of unaccounted mails is a bi-annual enumeration exercise taken up in all delivery post offices from 8th to 21st February/and between the same dates in August every year. The number of articles obtained in these four weeks is then multiplied by a factor of 10.714 (65 days deducted for Sundays and holidays and remaining 300 days is divided by 28 days which gives a figure of 10.714) to arrive at total traffic of each kind of articles handled during the year. This data so collected is invariably found to be on the higher side, and has to be deflated by comparing it with the estimates on revenue receipts. It is understood that the scaling down is to the extent of about 70 per cent so as to be compatible with revenue figures. In case of the time factor, the same was devised by the Department more than 40 years back. Though some revision has taken place after large scale computerization of operations in the post offices, the revised time factor is still to be used for estimating costs. For example, the time factor for a money order for the purpose of calculating cost is taken as 7.5 minutes based on manual operations involved in booking of a money order (3.5 minutes), payment of money orders (2.5 minutes) and miscellaneous items regarding documentation. With computerization, the booking of money order can be done in less than 2 minutes and the entire operation should take about 2 to 3 minutes only. Consequently, the cost of handling a money order which is shown as Rs. 53.20 (year 2003-04) would be much lower. Similar would be the case in respect of other products/services whose operations have been computerized. Thus, the time factor based on computerized norms would significantly alter the allocation of expenses on all the products/services and consequently their costs. For these reasons, there is a case for reviewing the costing methodology followed presently by India Post.

Moreover, as the products/services offered by India Post are not supply determined like electricity, it does not make sound economic reasoning to allocate the entire expenditure on the cost of the products. This is especially so in the current scenario of falling demand of some products such as ordinary mail volume, registered letters, parcels, etc. The existing methodology of calculating costs will only show increases in costs of products/services and would not reflect the existence of idle capacity/surplus resources in the system. In fact, as a result of this costing methodology, what is happening is a graveyard spiral of increasing prices for some products and consequently declining market share. This pricing policy is leading into a form of cream skimming, where the organization is losing business in lucrative segments (for example, between metros) and increasing business in segments where it is incurring loss. This method of allocating expenses is raising the cost of products such as parcels, registered letters, etc., whose traffic is falling, and thus, instead of reducing prices of these products in order to make them more competitive, there is actually a pressure to increase their prices. Also the present methodology does not reflect actual utilization of the resources. For example, the entire network cost is taken into account for working out the cost of non-USO products, though they are not being delivered in the rural areas. Consequently, it has the effect of increasing the cost of a non-USO product like speed post thereby making out a case for reducing its price becomes, so much more difficult.

Not surprisingly, the Demands for Grants of the Department have been repeatedly showing an uncovered deficit. For the year 2006-07, it was Rs. 1249.52 crore. Actual deficits as per Appropriation Accounts 2005-06 for the previous five years were Rs. 1209.88 crore 2005-06), Rs. 1381.84 crore (2004-05), Rs. 1375.22 crore (2003-04), Rs. 1364.40 crore (2002-03), Rs. 1411.51 crore (2001-02). Further, the Annual Report of the Department for the year 2006-07 showed that on the basis of the actual data for the year 2003-04, except for two products, namely, insurance and foreign mails, all other 18 products incurred losses. The average costs of these 18 products were substantially more than their respective average revenues. Even speed post showed an average cost of Rs. 44.54 against average revenue of Rs. 36.08. The figures for parcel were Rs. 80.94 and Rs. 57.17 respectively. This kind of a situation makes pricing decisions critical for survival of India Post. What is required, therefore, is an appropriate pricing methodology which should be based on carefully identified and computed costs.

5.3 New Approaches to Costing and Pricing

It is widely recognized that there is a need for a total paradigm shift by India Post in matters relating to costing and pricing. This would essentially require maintaining data pertaining to actual, showing available manpower, utilization of manpower on each of the activities; data on weight, volume, distance, origin-destination segment-wise, customer-wise, etc. The data should be so maintained that they become a part of a day-to-day activity of a post office. It can either be maintained on a census basis, or on a sampling basis, so as to give estimates on actual consumption of factors of production in delivering a product/service.

The problem of pricing in India Post arises from the fact that it produces several products involving joint costs. There is, therefore, a need to classify the costs as attributable to a product and those costs, which can be termed as joint costs. Cost should be attributed if it can be directly linked to a product, or it can be causally linked with volume related mail characteristics that can be used as a distribution key (e.g. weight). It can also be reasonably assigned if: (i) it can be causally linked with a non-volume related mail characteristics (e.g. delivery service standard); and (ii) a suitable distribution key can be developed for allocating the functional costs to classes and services. Those costs which cannot be causally linked with any specific mail characteristics, or a suitable distribution key simply cannot be developed can be termed as residual costs or joint costs. Further, mail characteristics with relatively high value of service should continue to reflect that higher value in their residual costs contribution, all other considerations being equal (for example higher residual costs for Speed Post).

Any pricing scheme should be such that each class of product must bear the direct and indirect cost attributable to the class, plus a portion of remaining institutional costs. One such pricing option is the Fully Distributed Costs Pricing method (F.D.C.). The FDC uses the ratio of: (a) attributable cost to a product to the total attributable cost [Attributed Cost Method (ACM)], or (b) output of a product to the total output [Ratio of Output Method (ROM)] or (c) revenue from a product to the total revenue [Ratio of Revenue Method (RRM)], to the joint costs for allocating the portion of joint costs which could be ascribed to that product. More recently some regulatory agencies have begun using price elasticity of demand in setting F.D.C. prices.

The literature on pricing shows that in the case of several products involving joint costs cross subsidy free prices based on ACM lead to optimal pricing of the products/services. India Post, however, is not following any of the above three methods but is using a modified version of ROM where the output is multiplied by the time factor to work out the ratio to be applied to joint costs.

No data is maintained which may enable some part of the joint costs to be attributed directly to the products. For India Post to follow an optimal pricing policy, i.e. cross subsidy free pricing based on attributable cost method, it would require estimates on: (i) attributable cost consisting of actual consumption of manpower costs and other inputs' costs for each product/service and also other costs like capital, printing, stationery, etc. and (ii) joint overhead cost. While calculating attributable cost, efforts would have to be made to include at least about 70 per cent of total cost as attributable cost, as is the practice followed by most postal administrations.

5.4 A Possible Model of Cost Allocation

For calculating attributable costs, India Post can try the Activity Based Costing (ABC) method. Because ABC focuses on the drivers and the fixed costs, it would lead to better forward looking costs. Its effect would be to reduce the pool of common (un-allocable) costs by tracing more of them through activities to different postal service/products. The ABC system would entail the following procedures:

(a) Activities must be properly identified and defined so as to create detailed process maps and activity dictionaries.
(b) Estimate the cost of each of the defined activities.
(c) Identify the cost drivers for each activity, i.e. how much of each activity is consumed by each product/services.

The requirement of data for ABC system is totally different from the data which is being presently maintained by India Post. India Post would, therefore, have to initiate efforts in this direction.

For purpose of illustration, a case study for only one product, namely Speed Post was taken up. One objective was to determine the data requirements of the ABC system. This case study was undertaken in one of the postal divisions, namely Aurangabad postal division of Maharashtra in January 2007. The procedure which was followed is given below:

(i) The steps involved in booking a speed post article in the office of booking, and its dispatch from that office of booking were listed (given in Appendix I of this chapter).
(ii) Also listed were the steps involved for delivering the speed

post article in the office of delivery, from the stage of receipt of the article in that office (given in Appendix II of this chapter).

(iii) A questionnaire was prepared for the Post Office staff to keep record of time taken for each of the steps involved in providing speed post service, and other services [the sample questionnaire is in Appendix III (of this chapter) which is only illustrative in nature, and does not claim to be exhaustive for the purpose of recording data].

(iv) Post Offices were chosen for the purpose of recording the data by following a random sampling method (given in Appendix IV of this chapter).

(v) The postmasters of those randomly selected post offices were called for a briefing to ensure a meaningful recording of data. The purpose of recording the data, i.e., for estimating the cost of providing the different postal services was explained, and they were asked to keep record of data for a period of one month.

However, the outcome of the survey clearly indicated that data were not entered on a day-to-day basis and that in most of the cases the questionnaires appeared to have been arbitrarily filled and returned. It was discovered that (i) the data were found to be internally inconsistent in the sense that in many cases the time recorded was more than the work norm time, (ii) it could be directly co-related with the existing establishment norms. Evidently, there seemed to be a general misconception amongst the employees regarding the objective of the exercise. In other words, data were not compatible with the requirements of ABC.

Not withstanding the outcome of the survey, ABC can be used for calculating costs of services. This would require a multi-stage cluster sampling for identifying post offices where record of data can be kept for the purpose of ABC analysis. In order to ensure that the data meet the requirements of ABC, a close interaction between the postal officials and outside professional investigators would be necessary.

The time taken on performing a particular activity for a product/service, multiplied by man-hour cost would give the direct labour cost component of that product/service. To this direct manpower cost, the cost of stationery and other elements of direct cost would be required to be added. ABC would still leave a significant cost, called facility sustaining cost, un-apportioned to the products. As price has to be based on the consideration of recovery of these costs also, the product price will have to be determined by adding mark-up on the costs ascertained on the basis of ABC. The mark-up can be decided in several ways.

(1) A uniform mark up can be applied to all the products to obtain a specified return on investment.
(2) A variable mark up can also be considered, for example, lower mark up for products under U.S.O. However, this will necessitate a higher mark up on premium products which may lead to non-competitive prices.
(3) Other pricing strategies which are product specific can also be considered, viz., for a new product it can be a market penetration strategy where the price at the beginning is deliberately kept low to capture the market.

By using the procedure described above, surplus capacity in the system can also be calculated. For the budget period the recorded data on traffic multiplied by standard time arrived through this procedure (ABC) can be compared with normal work hours. Normal hours available, less the actual hours utilized is the measure of surplus capacity. The surplus capacity in hours can then be converted into monetary terms on multiplying this by the average cost of one man-hour to give an estimate of idle capacity cost.

ABC will always be inadequate as a sole means of setting postal prices, because other factors such as prices prevailing in the market, etc., would also need to be taken into consideration. It cannot be justified, if designed purely with the product costing system to support pricing. However, properly designed ABC system will improve the manner in which costs are traced to individual postal prices. It undoubtedly increases the attributable portion of fixed cost which, in turn, will reduce the common cost pool. The residual portion of joint costs which cannot be allocated to any of the products can be apportioned using the ACM for deciding the cross-subsidy free pricing. Thus the ABC will be a better system than the one presently being followed.

(One disadvantage of fully distributed cost pricing is that being cost based it does not encourage cost minimization. In fact it would induce cherry picking by the competitors. Even so purely cost based prices have been advocated for practical considerations. It can be improvised by using "pertinent stand alone cost", which is not the actual or total cost incurred by the incumbent, but rather an estimate of the cost that would be incurred by a hypothetical commercial firm).

5.5 USO Products/Services

Because of USO in India Post, a cross subsidy free pricing strategy would not be possible for all the services/products. For those services being provided to fulfil the USO, the pricing strategy would necessarily be different from the competitive products. This is because an important prerequisite of USO is that prices should be affordable (and also uniform). In case of India Post, there is a vast rural network of post offices not justified on grounds of technical efficiency/income. This study revealed varying estimates of surplus post offices: (i) 1,04,261 in global comparison, (ii) 1,05,509 in Asian comparison, (iii) 1,11,565 in emerging economies comparison, and (iv) 42,142 in intra-comparison of circles. Evidently, these post offices have to be continued in order to fulfil the USO. A uniform price for USO services based on cross-subsidy free pricing, i.e. after incorporating the cost of maintaining these surplus post offices, may not be affordable.

The cost of the USO, therefore, cannot be entirely recovered from the prices of USO products/services. However, before exploring alternative ways of recovering the cost of USO, there is a need to have reliable estimates of cost of USO. The two methods of calculating the cost of USO (COUSO) are: the Net Avoided Cost (NAC) method and the Entry Pricing Method. The Net Avoided Cost (NAC) method calculates cost of USO as the decrease in the loss of revenue by withdrawing the service (in case of activity definition) and by withdrawing the product (in case of product definition). As all products listed in First Schedule (i.e., in respect of which prices are revised by Parliament) are being made available to the rural and far-flung areas it may be construed that India Post is following the activity definition of USO. Thus, according to this definition the cost of the USO would be equal to the expenditure saved by India Post on closing down all loss making post offices in these areas (under NAC method).

The cost of USO under certain assumptions (as discussed below regarding expenditure and revenue of rural post offices) using the NAC method is calculated as follows:

NAC = Net Average annual expenditure on allowances and other miscellaneous. expenses (i.e., net of average annual earnings from these post offices).
★ Total no. of post offices found surplus.

Average annual expenditure can be taken as Rs. 65,000 per annum [@ Rs. 3000 per month as allowance for one employee and assuming one employee in about 25 per cent of post offices and more than one employee (two employees) in remaining post offices, and Rs. 1,000 as miscellaneous expenditure].

As most of the post offices are not earning even 20 per cent of the cost (with most earning 5 to 10 % of their cost), an average estimate of income would be Rs. 10,000 per annum.

Therefore, the net expenditure can be taken as Rs. 55,000 per annum. Accordingly, the estimates of NAC would therefore be: (i) Rs. 573 crore in case of global comparison; (ii) Rs. 580 crore in case of Asian comparison; (iii) Rs. 614 crore in case of emerging economies; and (iv) Rs. 232 crore in case of circle comparison. [We also note that there is no reliable data available to calculate the cost of USO under the entry pricing method (EP) which is the loss in revenue to India Post as a result of liberalization of market].

The cost of USO can be covered through a combination of reasonable prices, cross-subsidy from profitable operations, direct subsidies from the government, and/or through the USO fund. The case for a USO fund is strong because India Post is no longer operating as a monopoly so as to entirely cross subsidize the cost of the USO. These subsidies/USO Fund may be used to determine the extent to which the prices of USO products/services could be kept below the costs.

Once the prices of USO products/services are fixed, the rates can be revised at periodic intervals thereafter depending upon the general conditions prevailing in the economy. A general principle for revision of such rates which is normally being followed by most of the postal administrations is the following:

$$PCR = CPI - X + Z$$

where PCR is Price Cap Regulation, CPI is Consumer Price Index, 'X' factor is (normally taken as) the rate of growth of total factor productivity, and 'Z' factors are exogenous factors such as changes in taxes, prices of critical inputs, which are beyond the control of the organization. The PCR provides an upper ceiling to the increase in prices which may be necessitated by the postal operators.

In case of India Post, prices of USO products (those products listed in First Schedule of the Indian Post Office Act in respect of which prices are revised by Parliament) have not been revised for several years, as can be seen from Table 5.1 given below.

Table 5.1: Postal Product Prices—Dates of Last Revision in Tariffs

Sl. No.	*Name of Service*	*Date of Last Revision of Tariff*
1.	Post Card	01.06.2001
2.	Printed Post Card	01.06.2002
3.	Com. Post Card	01.06.2002
4.	Letter Card	01.06.2002
5.	Letter	01.06.2002
	REGISTERED NEWSPAPER	
6.	Single	01.06.2001
7.	Bundle	01.06.2001
	BOOK POST	
8.	Book Pattern and Sample Packets	01.06.2002
9.	Printed Books	01.06.2001
10.	Other Periodicals	01.06.2002
11.	Parcel	01.06.2002
12.	Registration	01.06.2001
13.	Value Payable Post	26.05.1999
14.	Insurance	31.08.1998
15.	Money Order	31.08.1998
16.	T.M.O.(Telegraph Money Order)	01.02.2002
17.	I.P.O.(Indian Postal Order)	26.05.1999
18.	Foreign Post	01.02.1999
19.	Acknowledgement	01.06.2001

Subsequent to the last revision in prices shown above, the Consumer Price Index (CPI) has gone up substantially. Increase in CPI directly impacts the expenses of the Department, as salary is the major component of cost which increases on account of increase in Dearness Allowance (DA) rates. A price freeze on these items which is presently continuing can be justified only on the grounds that the rate of increase in inflation has been taken care of by the rate of increase of productivity in the Department. But this has not been so: in fact, our study shows that productivity in India Post has remained more or less stagnant and may have marginally declined. Thus, there is a strong case for India Post to revise the prices of USO products.

Even otherwise, India Post has reason for revising prices of some of the extensively subsidized products such as Registered Newspapers (both single and bundle) where the costs do not even cover the increased cost of transport. Newspapers earn mainly from commercial advertisements; so if the rates of advertisements have gone up in the last 4-5 years then India Post should logically go for raising tariff of registered newspapers.

Advertisement rates of some of the newspapers collected, revealed the following: (i) in case of Tarun Bharat, the commercial rate of advertisement per column cm was Rs. 100 in the year 2001 and it doubled to Rs. 200 per column cm subsequently; (ii) in case of *Dainik Jagran*, the DAVP (Directorate of Audio Visual Publicity) rate of *Dainik Jagran* was Rs. 25.64 per column cm in 2002 and it increased to Rs. 32.84 in 2004; (iii) in case of *Hindustan Times*, the DAVP rate was Rs. 17.26 in 2003 and it increased to Rs. 24.34 in 2004. As the advertisement rates of the newspapers did go up, India Post should have increased the rates of delivering newspapers.

Moreover, the Report of the Working Group on Posts, Tenth Five Year Plan (Government of India, 2002) made an observation that concessional tariff for transmission of registered newspapers account for loss of Rs. 103 crores per year. In 1898 when the Indian Post Office Act was enacted, the Post Office was given the responsibility of looking after the development of the Fourth Estate by way of grant of concessional postal tariff to help them to stand on their legs. During the intervening period of more than 100 years there have been many developments. There is now a nodal Ministry In-charge of Information and Broadcasting, which has the responsibility of looking after the newspaper industry. In the circumstances, the question of transmission by post of registered newspapers at concessional rates should be taken care of by that Ministry. In fact a lot of operational problems have developed because of difference in definition of newspapers as laid down in the Indian Post Office Act (the term registered newspaper includes transmission by post of Weekly, Fortnightly, Monthly magazines and journals of any and every kind and not necessarily the daily newspapers) and the Act/Rules framed by the Ministry of Information and Broadcasting for managing the affairs of the newspaper industry. Subsidies for granting concessional postages for registered newspapers should be a subject, which should therefore be handled by the Ministry of Information and Broadcasting and the subsidies on this score, if any, should be paid for by the Ministry of Information and Broadcasting.

The above Working Group also estimated that the subsidy on account of transmission by posts of book packets containing printed materials accounted for about Rs. 40 crores per year. As the Ministry of Human Resource Development is the nodal Ministry for this, the question of subsidization of the same by way of postal concession would better be managed by that Ministry, and any decision for subsidization would get better consideration when it is handled by the latter.

5.6 Commercial (Premium) Products/Services

Commercial product/services must, in terms of both price and quality, have to be necessarily competitive with those provided by the private operators. There is, therefore, a need for the Post Office to have full autonomy in deciding the prices of such services. This will require a pricing strategy which will make these products competitive, and a management strategy to ensure appropriate incentives to generate business in competition with private players. A purely cost-plus price-based strategy alone will not work in the rapidly changing market scenario in which India Post is functioning. Within these constraints prices of premium services should be fixed such that they could partially or fully cross subsidize the universal services.

In order to make the above strategy workable and also to have clarity in costing of products, one way of going about it is to ensure that commercial services provided by India Post utilize resources which can be easily identifiable. For example, there can be separate manpower for providing these services; transportation can be outsourced; and even delivery of these services can be done exclusively either by postmen or by Extra Departmental Agents if possible. Residual costs such as space utilized by the commercial services in the Post Offices, general supervision cost, etc., however, would still need to be allocated.

The competitiveness of Speed Post product of India Post was examined with reference to products offered by some private couriers. Data on prices charged by some of the private couriers is given in Table 5.2.

Table 5.2: Comparative Tariffs Charged by Some Private Couriers *vis-à-vis* Speed Post (Rates as in June 2007)

Name of the Courier	*Local Rates*	*Domestic Rates*
Blue Dart	Rs. 42 (Up to ½ Kg)	Rs. 142 (Up to ½ kg)
DHL	Rs. 35	Rs. 123
First Flight Couriers Ltd.	Rs. 20	Rs. 25 (within state) Rs. 60 (Rest of India) for wt. 100 gms.
Tej Courier	Rs. 15	Rs. 48
India Post (Speed Post)	Rs. 12 (effective from 11.6.2007)	Rs. 25 (up to 50 gms. All India) Rs. 30 (for distance less than 1000 km) Rs. 50 (for distance more than 1000 km)

Though the rates of Speed Post were found to be very competitive, even then the private couriers do manage to take away bulk of corporate mails. This is because of their policy of giving liberal discounts on bulk products. Such a kind of a discount facility is also available in India Post but the provision of discount suffers from a major draw-back as the same cannot be given across the counter at the time of booking of the article. The customer is required to make an application for claiming discount at a later date. This discount cannot be paid immediately as the power to admit this claim does not vest with the postmaster but with the postmaster general of the circle who can only sanction this claim. There is, therefore, a need for an appropriate marketing strategy at the operational level to be devised by India Post to make it more competitive in the market.

5.7 Work Sharing and Access Pricing

In order to fulfil the USO, India Post is currently providing coverage to all the households in the country for the purpose of delivering mails through its postmen. Though the volume of mails has gone down, the postmen cover a fixed route for delivering mails on a daily basis. In a way, therefore, the establishment cost of postmen and other delivery agents is a fixed cost for the department. If the delivery network is thrown open to other competitors in the market on levying a tariff, this would bring in additional revenue to the department. A similar kind of model has been utilized by the telecommunication and other utility industries where the last mile segment has been thrown open to other competitors. An appropriate pricing scheme can be devised for the purpose. This would not only bring additional resources to the department, but would also save the resources of the economy in the form of network duplication, which is presently occurring. Cost Based access charge or some other pricing rule could be levied by India Post for delivering the product of the competitors/couriers.

Efficient Component Pricing Rule permits the network owner to charge the user a price equal to the direct per unit incremental costs of supplying the units (i.e. access) plus the incremental opportunity costs to the network owner of the sale of a unit. By this formula the price of access would include the profit that the network owner would have realized if owner had supplied the entire product on its own. An alternative is "clean slate bargaining framework" that does not raise an obligation by the entrant to include incumbent's opportunity costs (including forgone profits).

Another option is to give discount to the mailers who desire to use certain segments of the supply chain including the last mile segment. The discount paid to mailers that perform postal functions should be exactly equal to the costs existing incumbent would have incurred had it moved the mail through those portions of its system. It is important to point out that it is incumbent posts avoided costs that are relevant in calculation of the costs for discount used to determine access price. However, such a discount policy cannot be applied by India Post as postal prices are not free from cross subsidy. Since the cost of delivery in rural areas is higher than the cost of delivery in urban areas, and there is a universal service provision of charging an average price for carrying mails nation-wide, it implies that the access pricing policy must be designed in such a way that it does not encourage wasteful cherry picking by entrants created by such subsidized prices (i.e., entrants delivering mails in urban areas and handing over the mails to the incumbent for delivery in rural areas). The access price to be charged in such case (for delivery in rural areas) should be equal to the costs to be incurred by the incumbent operator in delivering that product in a given area. The basic idea is the Delivery Area Access Pricing which is to charge higher access price for downstream entry where such entry requires delivery to high costs areas. Thus the key is to charge entrant who bypass up-streams operations of the post office not according to the work they have bypassed, but according to the work to be performed in delivering the mail they repost with the postal operator.

5.8 Summary

The present system of pricing followed by India Post is to cost the products/services by allocating its expenses on them. The distribution of expenses of the department on these products/services is based primarily on their respective traffic, and time factor for handling the products. But data on ordinary mails is not reliable and is found to be on the higher side; it is scaled down to the extent of 70 per cent so as to make it compatible with their revenue figures. The time factor for the products/services was devised by the department more than 40 years back, and though some revision has taken place after large scale computerization of operations in the post offices, it is not being used for estimating costs. The costing methodology followed presently by India Post is, therefore, required to be reviewed. Further, in this existing methodology of costing, as the entire expenses are distributed amongst the products/services, so even with falling traffic the methodology does not reflect the idle capacity in the system. For these reasons there is a need to look at new methods of costing. The literature on pricing shows that in case of several products involving joint costs, the cross-subsidy free prices based on Attributable Cost Method (ratio of attributable cost to the product to the total attributable cost) leads to optimal pricing of the products/services. As India Post also produces several products involving joint costs, the result of a case study attempting to attribute joint costs using ABC method has been studied.

APPENDIX-I
Steps Involved in Booking and Dispatch of Speed Post Articles in Head Post Office

(1) Presenting of speed post article on counter by the customer.
(2) Verification of address and condition of speed post article by counter clerk.
(3) Weighing of the speed post article on weighing scale.
(4) Counter clerk will tell the exact amount of tariff to customer according to weight and distance.
(5) Customer will pay the amount of tariff or affix required postage stamps on article.
(6) Booking of article by counter clerk on computer with date and time.
(7) Pasting Barcode on the article.
(8) Presenting the generated receipt to customer with Barcode and date.
(9) Transfer of data entry of speed post articles booked to Speed Post Centre.
(10) Transfer of speed post article to Speed Post Centre.
(11) Sorting of speed post articles for National Speed Post Centres/State Speed Post Centres-wise.
(12) Preparation of dispatch manifest by Postal Assistant of Speed Post Centre by scanning the Barcode.
(13) Generating the dispatch manifest for each Centre.
(14) Preparation of bag for dispatch through Air/Railway Mail Service.
(15) Pasting bag barcode on each bag ready for dispatch.
(16) Preparation of Transit Bag/Mail Bag/Weigh Bill and to be dispatched by Air/Railway Mail Service or by Transit Mail Office, as per instructions.
(17) Conveyance of bags to Railway Mail Service Office/Air Port/Transit Mail Office by Auto or Mail Motor Service.
(18) Preparation of Abstract.
(19) Preparation and keeping of day-to-day record.
(20) Local delivery article to be sorted and preparation of

delivery list for postman by Postal Assistant (PA) Speed Post Centre.

(21) Uploading delivery status date through internet to Speed Post Central Server.

APPENDIX-II

Steps Involved in Delivery of Speed Post Articles

(1) Offloading of speed post bags from Mail Motor by Gr. D. official of Mail Branch.
(2) Conveyance of speed post bags from Mail Branch to Speed Post Centre by Gr. D.
(3) Receipt of speed post bags with mail list in Speed Post Centre by P.A. Speed Post Centre.
(4) Checking of bags by PA Speed Post Centre.
(5) Scanning of bag labels by P.A. Speed Post Centre.
(6) Opening of bags by P.A. Speed Post Centre.
(7) Checking of manifest received from inside the bag.
(8) Scanning of all Speed Post Articles received from the bag.
(9) Segregation of articles meant for other delivery offices attached to Speed Post Centre.
(10) Preparation of dispatch manifest for other delivery offices by Speed Post Centre PA.
(11) Dispatch to other delivery office through Auto/Mail Motor Service.
(12) Segregation of beat-wise articles to be delivered through Speed Post Centre (Delivery).
(13) Scanning of Speed Post articles (beat-wise).
(14) Generation of delivery slips.
(15) Noting down the returned Speed Post Articles after scanning.
(16) Taking information on telephone from the delivery offices about Speed Post articles, which are not delivered on the day.
(17) Preparation of abstract (generated from computer).
(18) Feeding of required information in track and trace system.

APPENDIX-III

DATE: ____________

1. Name of Post Office: [ ]

2. Status: HSG ☐ LSG ☐ A Class ☐ B Class ☐ C Class ☐

3. No. of Staff: SPM ☐ PA ☐ Postman ☐ Group D ☐

   For SO

   GDS MD/MC ☐

   For HO PM ☐ APM ☐ PA's ☐

   Combined delivery: Yes ☐ No ☐

   Postman (i) for accountable articles ☐

   Postman (ii) for ordinary articles ☐

4. No. of PA's at counters: ☐
5. Whether building: Departmental ☐

   Rented ☐
6. Area of the PO ☐ Sq. feet Rent per month Rs. ☐
7. No. of Speed Post articles booked: ☐

7(a) Actual time taken for booking one article: ☐ Minutes

8. No. of Registered articles booked: ☐

8(a) Actual time taken for booking one article: ☐ Minutes

9. No. of Parcels booked: ☐

9(a) Actual time taken for booking one article: ☐ Minutes

10. No. of EPP booked: ☐

10(a) Actual time taken for booking one article: ☐ Minutes

11. No. of Insured Letters/Parcels booked ☐

11(a) Actual time taken for booking one insured article ☐ Minutes

12. No. of VPL/VPP booked ☐

12(a) Actual time taken for booking one VP article ☐ Minutes

13. No. of Money Orders booked: ☐

13(a) Time taken for booking of MO: ☐ Minutes

14. No. of Telephone bills accepted: ☐
15. No. of MSEB bills accepted: ☐

15(a) Actual time taken for one bill: ☐ Minutes

16. No. of Transactions done:

	Deposit	Withdrawals
SB	☐	☐
RD	☐	☐
TD	☐	☐
MIS	☐	☐
Sr. Citizens	☐	☐

16(a) Actual time taken for doing One transaction

	Deposit	Withdrawals
SB	☐	☐
RD	☐	☐
TD	☐	☐
MIS	☐	☐
Sr. Citizens	☐	☐

17. No. of NSCs/KVPs/IVPs: Issued ☐ Discharged ☐

17(a) Actual time taken for one: Issued ☐ Discharged ☐ Certificate

18. No. of IPOs sold: ☐

19. No. of IPOs Paid ☐

19(a) Actual time taken for one IPO: Sold ☐ Minutes
Paid ☐ Minutes.

20. No. of PLI receipts issued: ☐

20(a) Actual time taken for issue of one PLI receipt: ☐ Minutes

21. No. of Money orders paid/issued: ☐ ☐

21(a) Actual time taken for one Money orders paid/issued ☐ ☐

22. No. of PLI payments: ☐

22(a) Actual time taken for one payment ☐

23. No. of Pension payment: ☐

23(a) Actual time taken for one payment: ☐ Minutes

24. No. of ordinary articles posted in the office for dispatch:

Envelopes	Inland Letters	Post cards	Book posts	News-Printed papers	Post cards
☐	☐	☐	☐	☐	☐

25. No. of LBs for clearance: ☐
No. of times of clearance: ☐

26. Total length of all delivery beats: ☐ Kilometer

27. No. of accountable articles received for delivery

Speed Post	Regd. Letters	Regd. Parcels	EPP
☐	☐	☐	☐

27(a) Time taken for delivery of each articles

Speed Post	Regd. Letters	Regd. Parcels	EPP

28. No. of ordinary articles received for delivery:

Envelopes	Inland Letters	Post cards	Book Posts	News-papers	Printed Post cards

28(a) Time taken for delivery of each articles:

Envelopes	Inland Letters	Post cards	Book Posts	News-papers	Printed Post cards

29. No. of staff doing back office work: PA ☐
Gr.D ☐

30. Suggestion/Comments:

APPENDIX-IV

Table I

Serial No	*Name of the Head Office*	*Pin Code Number*
1.	Aurangabad	431 001
2.	Jalna	431 203

Table II

Serial No	*Status*	*Name of the Office*	*Pin Code Number*
1.	HSG-II	Sillod	431 112
2.	LSG	Aurangabad Cantt.	431 002
3.		Chikalthana Ind. Area	431 210
4.		Cidco Colony	431 003
5.		Kannad	431 103
6.		Kranti Chowk	431 005
7.		Osmanpura	431 005
8.		Vaijapur	423 701
9.		Jalna R.S.	431 203

Table III

Serial No	*Status*	*Name of the Office*	*Pin Code Number*
1.	Class-I	Gangapur	431 109
2.		Chikalthana	431 201
3.		S. Colony	431 001
4.		Bhokardan	431 114
5.	Class-II	Aurangabad City	431 001
6.		Ellora	431 102
7.		Lasur Stn	431 702
8.		Nizamganj	431 001
9.		Samarth Nagar	431 001
10.		Waluj	431 133
11.		Jafferabad	431 206
12.		Shivna	431 132

Table IV

Serial No	*Status*	*Name of the Office*	*Pin Code Number*
1.	Class-III	Badod Bazar	431 134
2.		High Court Building	431 005
3.		Harsool	431 110
4.		Nathnagar North	431 106
5.		Paithan SK	431 148
6.		Raghunathnagar	431 101
7.		Vaijapur Town	431 701
8.		A.M. Jalna	431 203
9.		C.C. Jalna	431 203
10.		Jalna I.E.	431 203
11.		Phardapur	431 118
12.		Wadigodri	431 205
13.		Sillod SK	431 135

Table V

Serial No	Name of the Sub-Office	Name of the Branch Office
1.	Aurangabad Cantt	Ghanegaon
2.	Badod Bazar	Pimpalgaon Kolta
3.		Shekta
4.	Chincholi Limbaji	Nevpur
5.	Deogaon Rangari	Tadpimpalgaon
6.	Bidkingaon	Dhorkingaon
7.		Sheota
8.	Chikalthana	Dudhad
9.		Pimpri
10.	Harsool	Jatwada
11.	Kannad	Chapaner
12.		Nagad
13.	Khultabad	Kagzipura
14.	Lasur Stn	Ghodegaon
15.	Nathnagar South	Changatpuri
16.	Pachod	Khadegaon
17.	Paithan SSK	Katpur
18.	Parsoda	Palkhed
19.	Phulambri	Pathri
20.	Pishore	Sarola
21.	Shiver	Kolhi
22.	Vaijapur	Chinchadgaon
23.		Nagamthan
24.	Akluj	Shendurwada

Serial No	Name of the Office	Name of the Branch Office
1.	Jalna H.O.	Dongaon
2.		Nava
3.		Shindekelgaon
4.	Ambad	Hatteokharni
5.	Ashti	Kekat Hadgaon
6.	Badnapur	Kandhari
7.	Banoti	Wadgaon Tigzi
8.	Bhokardan	Bhabulgaon
9.		Adegaon
10.	Jafferabad	Bharaj
11.	Kumbhar Pimpalgaon	Mangrul
12.	Mantha	Khirala
13.	Partur	Pangari Gosavi
14.	Ranjani	Jiradgaon
15.	Shivna	Adgaon
16.		Warud Tangda
17.	Sillod	Mangrul
18.	Sillod SSK	Nillod
19.	Tembhurni	Kumbharzari
20.	Wadigodri	Shahipur

6

Policy Implications

6.1 Introduction

The study on productivity and efficiency of India Post with reference to the developing economies show that the projected point for India Post on the production frontier is a point which is a convex combination of the points represented by Brazil (with weight 0.108), China (with weight 0.756), and Korea (Dem. Republic—with weight 0.136) on the frontier. This projected point for India Post is closest to China. In the context of Asian Economies too, this projected point of India Post on the frontier is closer to China and in the study of emerging economies it is closer to both Brazil (0.376) and China (0.624). Some of the policies followed by China and Brazil would, therefore, be relevant for India Post. We now attempt understanding these policies amongst others from the point of view of reforms in India Post.

6.2 Productivity and Efficiency: Lessons from other Countries and Implications

In order to fully exploit the growing postal market and also to effectively compete in the market, postal services in both China and Brazil have been drastically restructured and reorganized during the last decade. China Post has been restructured as state-owned enterprise with setting up of China Post Group (CPG) in December 2006 with registered capital of 80 billion yuan (about 11.5 billion dollars) and Brazil's postal service has been restructured as a state company, namely, Empresa Brasileira de Correios e Telegrafos

(Brazilian Post and Telegraph Company) commonly referred to as ECT. Currently, India Post is a part of the Government with the annual budgetary exercise requiring approval of Parliament for incurring expenses and fixing tariffs. This process is too long drawn out and cumbersome and, therefore, makes it virtually impossible for India Post to compete effectively in the market. It is, therefore, suggested that India Post needs to restructure itself in such a way which can give the organization operational freedom in competing and exploiting the opportunities in the market. It may not be possible for India Post to function as a full-fledged state owned enterprise having authorized capital unless the large number of post offices not justified on grounds of efficiency are either closed down, or if allowed to continue are financed separately. (It needs to be noted that though China has larger population and a bigger area than India, the number of post offices in China are less than half the number in India). Thus, to start, with it may be mandated that a fixed budgetary support is given to India Post on an annual basis with all operational freedom including decisions on investments and tariff fixation. There should also be a definite road map for India Post to move towards corporatisation.

The proposed organizational structure should enable India Post, like CPG, to launch subsidiaries to exploit the market. There can be separate subsidiaries for express services and private document services. These subsidiaries can enter into joint ventures with domestic and foreign companies to participate in lucrative international markets primarily intra-Asian express mail and package delivery. Some profitable units can then be packaged for limited IPOs to raise private capital.

India Post may consider setting up subsidiaries and joint ventures on priority to tap the domestic and global market in parcels and e-commerce. Parcel products together with e-commerce are a direct outcome of increasing demand in the economy. Presently, only a small percentage (11% in 2004) of income comes from parcels and logistics. E-commerce is a fast growing market due to on-line shopping. More and more firms are offering their products on-line. These range from gift cards/items and audio/video cassettes to books, magazines, and items of personal use such as clothes and accessories. With a vast network of offices especially in the semi-urban and rural areas under its command, India Post has a comparative advantage and monopoly in its reach. It can tie up with those organizations in the business of these goods to exploit and cater to the vast and immense potential of unfulfilled demand of the rural and the semi-urban populace. Like CPG, it can also build a nationwide business logistics operations. Alternatively, it can also tie-up with other logistics and supply chain management companies for providing interface with customers and for the last mile segment. Because of surplus capacity in the system, as revealed from the studies, India Post can operate either on a variable cost principle and/or on a cost plus principle, both of which would contribute to a decrease in its deficits.

However, to effectively compete in the market, it is suggested that India Post should transform its country-wide postal services from a labour-intensive industry to a technologically efficient service, networking and integrating all postal outlets. China conceived the postal integrated network in 1999 and currently has on the network 37,000 IT-enabled postal outlets (each also offering financial services). In contrast, India has only about 10,000 computerized offices with networking of about 1200 offices. India Post should, therefore, launch a massive programme of computerizing and networking all its offices on priority. The programme to computerize and network all its 25,800 departmental offices and 64,000 branch post offices in the Eleventh Plan should be expedited.

With this proposed computerizing and networking, India Post can start a range of value-added and e-enabled services, like China and Brazil. These can be video-phone conference system, EMS system, and agency businesses. In fact, on the foundation of its extensive and ubiquitous network of 1.55 lakh post offices, India Post like CPG and ECT can reinvent itself as a "bank of services", contracting its distributional infrastructure to other governmental agencies and private businesses—bill processing, tax registration, online access, forms and documents, auto registration, passports, voting, collecting fees, and more. The network can also be leveraged and used as a conduit to bring small loans, insurance, ATMs, and Internet transfers into the back country. These measures can bring in substantial revenue to India Post, like Brazil where these contract services amount to over 20 per cent of ECT revenues.

It is found that the last three years have seen an explosion in non-mail services provided by CPG and ECT—primarily banking and financial services. Such services are closely linked to industrial development and are profitable for CPG. ECT and Brazil's largest bank, Banco Bradesco, entered into a joint venture whereby

Bradesco could use the post offices as bank branches, especially in remote areas offering deposits, loans, credit cards, bill payment, direct deposit, tax and social security payments as well as phone and internet banking on Bradesco's network. Through joint ventures and contracts India Post can also move aggressively into banking services of all kinds and may also think of setting up its own more closely held banking operation. Bulk of revenues can come from the banking ventures as in case of Brazil. India Post can also consider updating its remittance system so that migrants from rural areas can use its network to send remittances back to their inland families. Presently, the annual remittance of Rs. 7757 crore in 2006-07 is too small compared to the estimated $30 billions (approximately Rs. 1,20,000 crore) in case of China.

Life insurance sales represent the next business venture for India Post. It can target farmers, low income urban residents, and migrant workers in particular. The Rural Postal Life Insurance (RPLI) which started in 1995, needs to be further strengthened, if need be, by setting up a company, on the same pattern as CPG which has formed a subsidiary called China Post Life Insurance Company Limited.

There is also an urgent and pressing need for India Post to redefine its Universal Service Obligations. As per Universal Postal Convention, Universal Postal Service is defined as the permanent provision of quality basic postal services at all points in a member country's territory, for all customers, at affordable prices. Presently, India Post has not identified products which can be labeled as USO products, such as in case of Brazil where the USO products (on which there is monopoly) consists of letters, postal cards, small parcels, telegrams and special mail bags. USO has been defined in the Outcome Budget, Department of Posts, 2006-07 as: ".... committed to fulfilling the Government's Universal Obligation in terms of providing basic postal services throughout the country, irrespective of terrain, at an affordable price." For this it has set up a large network of 1,55,204 post offices (as on 31.3.2007) of which 1,27,062 are Branch Post Offices catering exclusively to the villages for ensuring: (i) daily delivery of dak at the doorstep of every customer anywhere in the country; (ii) collection of letters; and (iii) for sale of stamps and stationery. It is, therefore, quite apparent that India Post is following the 'activity' definition of USO. For clarity on USO, and for sustainability of the organization India Post need to define some products as USO products, on which it may have monopoly and which may be subsidized.

Survival of any organization in a competitive environment requires a level playing field. In case of India Post this kind of level playing field is lacking, as India Post is having a USO burden which is not being shared by other private service providers. This is leading to a graveyard spiral of increasing prices of products offered by India Post and consequently decreasing market share (of India Post). Its competitors have gained significantly by allowing them to have the benefit of cream-skimming. Healthy competition necessitates that this USO burden on India Post should also be shared by other private service providers. Countries like Brazil and China maintain a reserve area. ECT maintains that the monopoly is not a privilege, but a "financing mechanism" to fund the nation's universal service requirement throughout Brazil's huge hinterland. In case of Brazil for the ECT to fulfil the universal service requirement, each postal operator is also assessed 0.5 per cent of its revenues for a fund for postal service universalization. Not surprisingly, it claims not to have received direct subsidies from the government since 1986. In case of China there is a legal monopoly on mail and parcels weighing 350 grams or less. It is also seeking a legislation for giving sole authority to handle documents weighing less than 150 grams. It is also pushing for increased taxation of foreign and domestic competitors in the express mail service market to support traditional mail. It is, therefore, suggested that India Post should be adequately compensated for the USO, either through a reserve area over which it can have a monopoly, or by levying USO fee on private postal operators. Different ways of financing the USO fund could be through cess on service tax payment, through a system of licensing of private operators in mail/parcel services or through an additional charge to be paid by the Couriers/Parcels/Logistics Companies. It can also be mandated that a certain percentage of the annual profit of all such companies could be contributed to the USO fund.

In this context, a current practice in the telecom sector in India which is also under similar kind of obligations needs to be pointed out. Earlier, provision of below-cost service in rural areas by the incumbent (Department of Telecommunication) was being taken care of by cross-subsidy from its profits. But with opening of the telecom market, prices of the incumbent also needed to be competitive. The USO, therefore, required to be supported by an "access deficit charge" paid both by entrants, i.e., private operators as well as incumbent, to the incumbent as compensation for its historical (existing) provision of services in high-cost areas. Moreover, to facilitate further provision of USO, a USO Fund was created by law [Section 9A of The Indian Telegraph Act, 1885 incorporated under The Indian Telegraph {Amendment} Act, 2003] to which a certain percentage (5% of adjusted gross revenue) is being contributed by all telecommunication service providers. These Universal Service Funds (USF) go to the Department of Telecommunication, which distributes them on the basis of auction for funding the USO programme, i.e., for setting up of more village public telephones, rural exchanges (Short Distance Charging Areas). A similar kind of USO fee should also be charged on private postal operators so that the cost of the USO is not borne entirely by India Post.

In the interest of long term sustainability of any solution, there would be a need for an independent agency which would decide on the cost of USO and the amount to be contributed by different postal operators towards the USO fund for financing the USO. Such a Regulatory Authority or a Postal Rate Commission are existing in several countries. In case of China, the State Postal Bureau itself had a dual role—it was both the regulatory authority on all postal matters and the organization which delivered the mail. But in 2006 the postal regulatory functions were separated and the State Post Management Bureau was set up as the agency which regulates postal services nationwide. The proposed Regulatory Authority while deciding the contribution for USO fund would need to see that the prices to be charged for basic services as part of USO services are reasonable, and are based on correct and appropriate costs of providing these services.

However, some issues need special consideration while deciding the extent of subsidy for the USO. As the information on cost would determine the subsidy for existing un-remunerative post offices, the incumbent may try to gain by manipulating how cost information is aggregated across service categories and across high-cost and low-cost areas. Further, as the cost of operation would be subsidized there might not be any incentive to reduce cost/improve efficiency. Even taxation of revenue to meet the USO would be inefficient. This is because as the price elasticity of demand is much greater for the products of couriers than that of products provided as universal service, taxing usage to finance the universal service would substantially distort the former to obtain very little gain in the latter. Subsidizing rural areas simply because they have high costs is not implied by optimal pricing, unless rural customers generate a much greater subscription externality than do urban subscribers.

At a disaggregated level, i.e. at the level of postal circles, Kerala and Haryana are the two circles which are peers to most of the circles. The productivity and efficiency in Kerala is better primarily because of a large volume of mail business which is generated on account of high level of literacy in the State. Further, Kerala has limited employment potential in comparison to its high literacy, causing migration of literate people to other parts of the country, and also to other countries. This generates substantial volume of business in terms of financial remittances and small savings. Similarly, the explosion of cities like Faridabad and Gurgaon in Haryana State has generated substantial mail volume, financial remittances and small savings. Accordingly, as a policy guideline it is suggested that other circles should also focus on increasing the small savings business, especially in the rural areas. They should also focus on improving its remittance service, which is increasing because of large scale migration of population due to growing urbanization of tier two and tier three cities.

Studies reveal that there has been a substantial decline in mail volume business in India Post in the last ten years from 1396 crore in the year 1995-96 to 646 crore in the year 2006-07. India Post, therefore, need to focus on increasing its mail volume business. Empirically, it has been established that the economic and demographic factors combined with marketing and sales activities and product innovations are the most important group of drivers which can offset the erosion of total mail volumes by new technology (Nankervis *et al.*, 1999). Particularly, India Post should concentrate on business and financial sectors which have potential for billing, financial statements and direct mail advertisements. Direct Mail, in particular, has enormous potential for growth as it is one of the several choices available to firms for communicating with customers. Santos *et al.* (2001) while studying the demand for direct mail in Portugal using a profit function found empirical evidence of negative relationship between demand and price. India Post should, therefore, follow appropriate strategies to increase its market share based on product innovation, improvement in quality of services, marketing activities, and pricing policies based on a combination of low prices and discounts.

6.3 Pricing Guidelines

As a pricing policy India Post should follow the policy of cross subsidy free prices as they are pareto optimal. This would necessarily require a change in methodology of costing based on accurate estimation of costs. ABC method for attributing fixed costs is recommended. However, underlying this change is a very important requirement in terms of maintaining the relevant data so as to enable accurate costing of products. It would be desirable to have a measure of work handled in a simple and continuous basis, which could be incorporated in day-to-day activities of the department. Such a system can be put in place in major offices and/or in offices, selected by random sampling.

Prices also need to be fixed based on market considerations. This would require estimates of demand functions together with demand elasticities, being key parameters in pricing decisions. Regular market surveys to have a good idea of the market structure and market share of each of the players for different products/ services, including the Post Office would also be required.

For effectively competing in the market, India Post may need to resort to differential pricing. Private companies have limited coverage with a structure of destination-based tariffs which are separate for local areas and proximate regions, metros and big urban centres to metros, and distant regions and hard to reach areas. For India Post tariffs are higher for local and metro/urban areas as compared to that offered by couriers. It is, therefore, suggested that India Post should consider reducing prices of products catering exclusively to the urban, metros and local markets. This is also justified because factors like postal density and other variables such as vertical concentration of houses (grouping index), reduce the cost of delivery (Roy, 1999, Scarfiglieri *et al.*, 2001). Donder *et al.* (2001) while studying the effect of fully liberalized market on uniform prices found that the spread of prices between that in the urban market and the rural area would range in the ratio of 5 to 6 times.

Moreover, pricing scheme consistent with cost-minimization and directed towards increasing the productivity and efficiency in the use of resources, necessitate full utilization of resources found in the surplus post offices. As these are in the nature of fixed costs, there is, therefore, a strong case for differential pricing based on the variable cost of performing the service. This would also help in reducing the deficits which for the year 2007-08 is Rs. 1511.44 crore.

India Post can also consider using access pricing as an option for offering the last mile segment to its competitors/private couriers because of large element of sunk costs in the delivery component of the postal value chain, especially in the rural areas. A study shows that if a competitor delivered mails six days a week and has a combined wage and efficiency advantage of 50 per cent, this competitor would have to capture 30 per cent of the total market in order to have the unit delivery cost equal to that of the existing postal operator (Bernard *et al.*, 2002). Most empirical studies have also confirmed increasing returns to scale/scope in mail distribution. The situation is somewhat similar to that found in the case of telecommunications or other utility services like electricity, where the last mile segment is thrown open to other competitors and for which tariff is charged by the existing incumbent. A case can, therefore, be made for controlling the last mile, that is, the essential facility, by the existing incumbent, i.e. India Post. Cost Based Access charge or some other pricing rule such as Delivery Area Access Pricing Rule could be levied by India Post for delivering the products of the competitors/couriers.

6.4 Summary

To sum up, a suitable restructuring of India Post is suggested, which can give operational freedom in deciding its investments and fixing prices. It would also enable India Post to set up subsidiaries for effectively competing and exploiting the opportunities in the market. Further, India Post needs to computerize and network all its offices, which would not only increase its competitiveness in the market but would also bring revenue by delivering all kinds of services of other organizations. India Post should also focus on banking and financial services, either by setting up its own full-fledged banking operations or through tie-ups with other banks. There is also an urgent need to define the USO products and find suitable ways of financing them so that India Post is not constrained in playing an effective role in facilitating economic growth.

7

Summary and Concluding Remarks

7.1 Summary

Productivity is defined as the ratio of total output to the amount of input used during the same period. This is the concept of Total Factor Productivity. However, a firm may not realize maximum output given inputs or, alternatively, may not use minimum input given output. Productivity may, therefore, vary not only due to differences in production technology but also due to differences in the efficiency with which inputs are converted into outputs. This brought in the concept of efficiency whereby the frontier approach to measurement of productivity was introduced. Total Factor Productivity is then defined as the net effect of change in inefficiency, movement along the frontier (scale economies), and shifts in the frontier, the latter being technical change.

Productivity and efficiency in the use of scarce resources are of immense concern in a developing economy like India. For postal administrations all over the world, the reasons for studying productivity and efficiency are even more pressing. Postal administrations are under a USO clause which makes it necessary for them to provide a minimum defined service to all persons at a uniform/affordable rate. Hitherto, they were fulfilling the USO through cross-subsidization of universal service. But with the opening of postal market the cross-subsidization of universal service is no longer possible. Postal administrations, therefore, need to focus more on increasing operational efficiency and productivity so as to enable them to preserve a fair and affordable postal rate for performing its universal service.

Review of the relevant literature revealed that some work has been done on estimating productivity and efficiency of postal administrations in advanced industrialized countries of Europe, USA, Australia, and Japan. But none of these models were found to be satisfactory. Outputs had been left out or wherever included, the outputs were not homogeneous to justify their aggregation (for example, aggregating mails and financial services). In some cases, the outputs were represented by revenue. Representing output by revenue require the behavioural assumption of revenue-maximization and observable (market) prices so as to reveal preferences of consumers. Such an assumption does not hold in case of a public postal operator because it is faced with several priorities and may not pursue the objective of revenue-maximization. For the same reason, any attempt to represent multiple output, multiple input features through a cost function is also not satisfactory because a public-postal operator may not pursue the objective of cost-minimization. Moreover, the dominant input, labour, is not paid wages based on marginal cost (but on average cost) and with high retention rates prevailing, it does not allow management to adjust labour in response to change in its prices so as to enable any meaningful interpretation of factor demand equations. This also makes using labour as an endogenous variable in a single input multiple output function model unrealistic. Because of these reasons findings based on estimated models of output represented by revenue, cost and input requirement functions would not give accurate results on productivity and efficiency. The Index number approach is also not suitable because it requires behavioural assumptions of cost-minimization and revenue-maximization. Further, it assumes all firms to be efficient and therefore, does not separate out technical progress from efficiency.

It was observed that in the case of India Post such studies were singularly missing except for one study by Jha *et al.* (1990) which used revenue to represent output. Productivity and efficiency of India Post is critical for its survival as India Post is facing diminished reserved areas due to opening of the postal market. Competition from private couriers in the market has also made pricing issues crucial. Because of these considerations, a study on productivity, efficiency, and pricing of India Post was necessitated. The objectives of the study are to see whether resources are being utilized in the most productive and efficient manner and also to examine a suitable pricing mechanism for the Department.

Measuring productivity and efficiency of any organization would be a simple exercise if the frontier production set was known. As it cannot be found in the blue prints of an engineer, it needs to be constructed from a sample of inefficient operations. That is why one uses the term "best practice" production set, made of those observations from the sample that appear to be the best ones in the sense of some posited assumption of dominance. For this reason, the choice of observations from relevant data becomes crucial.

The study is confined to India Post with reference to developing countries/emerging economies, and postal circles within India Post. The multiple output, multiple input technology is modeled using the distance function approach, which is a natural way of modelling production frontier, as also deviations from and shifts in that frontier. The Malmquist Productivity Index (MPI), which is constructed from distance functions, is estimated for measuring productivity and efficiency. This index is used because it requires neither price or share data allowing applications where outputs or inputs may not be marketable, nor behavioural assumption concerning revenue-maximization, cost-minimization, or profit-maximization. An output orientated model is chosen. The MPI is calculated by applying the linear programming method using Tim Coelli's DEAP version 2.1. The slacks in output and inputs have also been estimated using multi-stage DEA. But as this non-parametric frontier approach confounds measurement errors and random shocks with technical in-efficiency, a parametric stochastic frontier approach for measuring technical efficiency proposed by Aigner *et al.* (1977) is also used. The translog functional form is specified for the distance function with technical progress defined as a trend variable, and technical efficiency modeled to be changing with time. An attempt is also made to identify key variables explaining efficiency. For the purpose of parametric estimation Tim Coelli's FRONTIER version 4.1 is used. Several hypotheses are also tested for the validity of the model.

The study begins with a global comparison of the developing economies with reference to India Post, followed by comparison of India Post with the developing economies of Asia. Thereafter a study of the emerging economies, the E-7 (Brazil, China, India, Indonesia, Mexico, Russia and Turkey), which are perceived to outpace the G-7 (US, Japan, Germany, UK, France, Italy, and Canada) on virtually every economic parameter by 2050 is undertaken. The productivity and efficiency at the disaggregated level of India Post, i.e., of postal circles are also analyzed. The productivity and efficiency results have been linked with pricing decisions of India Post. Modality of deciding prices of postal products for India Post in the present era of competition in the postal market has also been discussed.

Data for the study in case of international comparisons have been taken from the Universal Postal Union's site. Data from the Book of Information and other official publications published by the Department of Posts, Government of India have been used for study on postal circles. All the outputs have been included in the study but they have been classified under broad categories. Only two inputs, namely, number of postal staff representing labour, and number of post offices representing capital have been taken.

In the study on international comparison of 23 developing countries for the period 2001-04, four output variables and two input variables are taken. Because of differences in prices of outputs, to facilitate international comparisons the outputs are weighted by their percentage income contribution to the total income. Results showed that total factor productivity change of India Post over the period remained stagnant with an average of 0.998. The average total factor productivity change of all the countries for this period is 1.048, i.e., a growth of 4.8 per cent, with countries such as Iran, Korea, Malaysia showing higher growth. Results also showed 1,04,261 surplus post offices in India, reflecting a typical case of stagnation in productivity with surplus capacity for India Post. This result is further confirmed in the Asian study of 11 countries—1,05,509 surplus post offices and a marginal decline in total factor productivity by 2.4 per cent.

In the study of India Post amongst the group of emerging market economies E-7, only three outputs and two inputs are considered. The data used for the study is for the period 1991-2005. Stagnation in productivity of India Post over these 15 years with excess capacity is again observed: total factor productivity change is found to be 1.005, with 45,532 surplus labour inputs and 1,11,565 surplus post offices.

In the stochastic frontier approach for estimating technical efficiency one of the outputs, namely, financial services is selected as the dependent variable and as the variable of normalization for other outputs. Most of the maximum likelihood coefficients are accurately estimated and are found to be significant. Technical inefficiency is correctly identified within the composed error term. Several hypotheses postulated to see whether the model adequately represented the data, are found to be valid. Results on technical efficiency showed that India Post ranked fourth amongst these seven emerging economies. A technical efficiency model regressed on two variables, namely, population per post office and mails per capita showed these two variables to be significant in explaining technical efficiency.

In the study of productivity and efficiency of India Post at the level of the postal circles, three outputs and two inputs are used. The stochastic frontier approach is used for estimating technical efficiency. Most of the parameters are found to be significant. The likelihood ratio test is also significant, confirming the hypothesis that technical inefficiency prevailing in the circles cannot be rejected. The mean technical efficiency of the circles is found to be 0.697. Non-parametric estimation using DEAP 2.1 version showed a decline in the mean technical efficiency of the circles from 0.845 in the year 1999 to 0.798 in the year 2004, assuming VRS 42,142 surplus post offices are also observed. The average total factor productivity is found to be 0.972 thus confirming the earlier conclusion derived from other samples (developing economies/emerging economies) that India Post is a case of stagnation/marginal decline in productivity, with surplus capacity.

The present system of pricing followed by India Post is to cost the products/services by allocating its expenses on them and then approach the Government/Parliament with a proposal for revision in prices. The distribution of expenses of the department on these products/services is based primarily on their respective traffic, and time factor for handling the products. But data on ordinary mails is not reliable and is found to be on the higher side. It is scaled down to the extent of 70 per cent so as to make it compatible with their revenue figures. The time factor for the products/services was devised by the Department more than 40 years back, and though some revision has taken place since then it is not being used in estimating costs. The costing methodology followed presently by India Post is, therefore, required to be reviewed. Further, in this existing methodology of costing, as the entire expenses are distributed amongst the products/services, even with falling traffic the methodology does not reflect the idle capacity in the system.

For these reasons there is a need to look at new methods of costing. The literature on pricing shows that in case of several products involving joint costs, cross-subsidy free prices based on Attributable Cost Method (ratio of attributable cost to the product to the total attributable cost) lead to optimal pricing of the products/services. As India Post also produces several products involving joint costs, the result of a case study attempting to attribute joint costs using ABC method has been reported. This data reported in study was found to be thoroughly inadequate and even inappropriate from the point of view of ABC system. A complete reorientation of the approach and methodology for data collection is suggested.

Studies show that a large number of surplus post offices in India Post are not justified on grounds of technical efficiency. Evidently, they are continuing in order to fulfil the USO of India Post. A cross-subsidy free pricing strategy incorporating the cost of maintaining these surplus post offices cannot be viable for the USO products/services because an important prerequisite of USO is that prices should be affordable (and also uniform). The cost of USO is, therefore, required to be calculated (which has been done using the NAC method) so that the same can be recovered through combination of reasonable prices, cross-subsidy from profitable operations, subsidies from the government, and/or through USO Fund. Thereafter, the rates can be fixed for these USO products/services, which can then be revised at periodic intervals commensurate with the increase in consumer price index after adjusting for the rate of growth of total factor productivity. It is observed that prices of those products which can be revised only by Parliament (i.e., those appearing in First Schedule and which may be construed as USO products/services in the absence of any concrete definition), have not been revised for several years. There is no justification for the existing price freeze on these items because there has been increase in Consumer Price Index, which has not been compensated by any increase in productivity of the department.

In the case of extensively subsidized products such as registered newspapers, the case for revision is very strong because advertisement rates of the newspapers have gone up substantively. Even then if a need is felt to subsidize this product, India Post should be compensated by the nodal Ministry looking after registered newspapers, i.e. the Ministry of Information and Broadcasting.

Similarly, the subsidy on book packets should be borne by the Ministry of Human Resource Development.

Commercial services have to be necessarily competitive with those provided by the private operators. There is, therefore, a need for India Post to have full autonomy in deciding the prices of such services. In order to make this strategy workable there is a need to have clarity in costing of products. One way of doing it is to ensure that the resources utilized by commercial services provided by India Post can be easily identified. Empirical analysis reveals that the rates of speed post are competitive but even then the private couriers manage to take away bulk of corporate mails. As this is because of the policy of giving liberal discounts on bulk products by the couriers, there is a similar need that the officials of India Post at lower levels be empowered to provide discounts to the customers.

India Post can consider introducing work sharing and offering last mile segment to the customers. An appropriate pricing scheme can be devised which would not only bring additional resources to the Department, but would also save the resources of the economy in the form of network duplication which is occurring presently. Cost based access charge or some other pricing rule could be levied by India Post for delivering the products of the competitors/couriers. While offering the last mile segment, care has to be taken to ensure that the cost of delivery is recovered. The access price in such cases should be equal to the costs to be incurred by the incumbent operator in delivering that product in a given area (Delivery Area Access Pricing).

Study of productivity and efficiency of India Post with reference to the developing economies, Asian and emerging economies show that projected point of India Post on the frontier is closest to China and Brazil, thereby implying that policies followed by these two countries would be relevant to India Post. As in the case of these countries, a suitable restructuring of India Post is suggested, which can give operational freedom in deciding its investments and fixing prices. It would also enable India Post to set up subsidiaries for effectively competing and exploiting the opportunities in the market. There is also a need for tapping the parcels and the e-commerce market. Further, India Post need to computerize and network all its offices, which would not only increase its competitiveness in the market but would also bring revenue by delivering all kinds of services of other organizations. India Post should also focus on banking and financial services either by setting up its own full-fledged banking or through tie-ups with other banks. India Post should also focus on generating more mail volume business for itself with focus on business and financial sectors, which generate more mails per unit of money on account of bills, financial statements and direct mail advertisements. There is also a need to redefine its universal service obligations so that only those products identified as USO products may be subsidized, while allowing the prices of remaining products to be determined by competition and market forces.

The burden of the USO should also be shared by other private service providers so as to give a level playing field to India Post. This may necessitate setting up a USO Fund which may be on the pattern of that in the Telecom sector; there could also be other ways of financing the USO Fund such as through system of licensing of private operators, cess on service tax payment, taxing annual profits of private couriers, etc. However, subsidizing USO products may not be implied by optimal pricing unless users of USO products generate a much greater subscription externality than the consumers of the non-USO products. Further, as estimates on cost of USO could be debatable, there is a need for an independent agency on the pattern of that existing in other countries to decide on both the USO Fund as well as the prices to be charged for postal services.

The pricing of non-USO products can be cross subsidy free prices which are Pareto-optimal. To ensure this, a change in the methodology of costing would be required which, in turn, would necessitate maintaining of relevant data. There could also be limitation on cost plus pricing because of competition with private service providers. There would thus be a need for pricing strategy based on market situations. This would require information on key parameters such as demand elasticities, demand functions, etc. India Post may also consider using the strategy of differential pricing, with lower prices to be charged for local areas, metros and from big urban centres. This differential pricing is justified because several studies have shown that the cost of delivery is much lower in areas with high density of population and households. One immediate way of implementing differential pricing is to provide discount to these products, which can be given across the post office counters. Availability of surplus post offices also makes a strong case for differential pricing based on variable cost principle.

7.2 Main Findings

The main findings of the study are summarized as follows:

(1) International comparison of India Post with reference to 23 developing economies for the period 2001-2004 showed that India Post reflects a typical case of stagnation in productivity with surplus capacity and idle costs.
(2) The above conclusion gets confirmed not only in the Asian study as well as in the study amongst the group of emerging market economies, but also at a disaggregated level, i.e. at the level of postal circles in India Post.
(3) Technical inefficiency was correctly identified within the composed error term with a very high share of technical inefficiency in total variance, thereby indicating that the vast majority of residual variation was due to the inefficiency effects.
(4) Mails per capita and population per post office were two regressors found to be significantly affecting technical efficiency.
(5) The existing costing methodology being followed by India Post has led to a vicious cycle of increasing prices and a declining market share for India Post. There is, therefore, a need for total paradigm shift in matters relating to costing and pricing.
(6) ABC is one option that can be tried for imputing the fixed costs to the product.
(7) There is a need to define USO products, the losses on which can be financed explicitly either through a USO Fund and/ or through budgetary support/recoveries. For remaining products, India Post needs to take a market sensitive approach to pricing.
(8) India Post can also try differential price based on variable cost, work sharing, and access pricing to bring in more revenue.
(9) The reimbursement to India Post in running the small savings scheme should also include an element of profit.

7.3 Concluding Remarks

A major limitation of the study was the lack of relevant and adequate data. For example, some countries such as South Africa, Ghana, Nigeria, which ought to have been included, had to be excluded from the study. Data also were required to be extrapolated to fill up the gaps (for example, in case of China data on savings bank had to be extrapolated as they were available for only four out of 15 years). Moreover, proxy variables for output had to be used (such as using number of savings accounts as substitute for number of savings bank transactions as one of the outputs for financial services). Important products such as Speed Post, retailing activities, etc. had also to be left out from the study due to lack of data. The results on productivity and efficiency, therefore, need to be seen keeping in view the above limitations of the study. A corollary of this is that there is a need for all postal administrations including India Post to maintain comprehensive and detailed records of data relating to products/ services and inputs used.

Another limitation of the study was that only two inputs (labour and number of post offices) were used. More inputs such as cumulative sums of annual investments less depreciation, number of equipments especially computers could have been considered. In fact, as computerization of postal operations is taking place across the board in all postal administrations, an attempt to analyze the effects of computerization on productivity would be an interesting study. However, this would also require that adequate, relevant and reliable data are available.

In the methodology followed for the study, firms may be dubbed as technically efficient and yet they may all be operating inefficiently. This is because the frontier set which is not known in reality is constructed using information from a sample of firms, and technical efficiency is measured/estimated in the context of the constructed frontier production set. Thus, if firms operate inefficiently but nonetheless are on best practice frontier, they will be dubbed technically efficient in this approach.

The time varying technical efficiency model chosen for the parametric method in our study does not account for situations in which some countries may be relatively inefficient initially but become relatively more efficient over time. This is because the technical inefficiency effects of different country at any given time period is specified to be equal to the same exponential function of the corresponding country specific inefficiency effect of the last period of the panel, thereby implying that the ordering of the countries according to the magnitude of technical inefficiency effects is the same for all periods. A different time varying technical efficiency model which overcomes this limitation on the fixed ordering of the countries according to the magnitude of technical inefficiency effects, may be taken up for further research.

The technical efficiency model used two explanatory variables, namely, population per post office and mails per capita in this study. Further research can include more variables for explaining technical efficiency such as: proportion of receipts devoted to investment; mailbox density (mailbox per 1000 km^2); inhabitants per mail box; human resource qualification; size of postal administration (as indicated by the number of letter post items); mails per delivery point; etc. However, as availability of data could be a major constraint, some assumptions may be required to be made. For example, in the case of human resource qualifications, the United Nations Development Programme Report figures on average years of study of people over 25 can be used as a proxy for postal workers' classification. The variable human resource qualifications can be further modified to that of index of capital which can be defined as combination of professional experience and education with suitable weights assigned to each.

Research can also focus on a more comprehensive methodology of costing of postal products. Cost of each of the components: collection, local transport, outward sorting, long overhaul transport, inward sorting, local transportation and delivery, can be estimated separately. This will enable India Post to unbundle its pricing so that each service component can be priced separately.

The transformation functions for each of these cost components can also be estimated. For example, in the case of collection and delivery functions in post offices, the variables can be the number of mail items delivered, number of workers, number of delivery points, area served, equipments such as mechanical vehicles, etc. The explanatory variables for efficiency could be the absentee rate, indicator of quality in delivery of mail (i.e., whether delayed at delivery post office after receipt), delivered mail per delivery point, etc. The study of other efficiency regressors and their contemporary and lagged effects can also be considered. There is a general agreement that mail transportation and sorting show constant returns to scale whereas the delivery shows increasing returns to scale. If this contention of returns to scale is validated by research work, then it has implication in terms of opening up transportation and sorting to competition, while maintaining monopoly in delivery.

Research can also focus on studying the cost elasticity of output relating to post office counter activities. This is especially important because retailing activities of post offices (for selling products of other organizations on commission basis or in collaboration) is being leveraged as one of the major sources for generating revenue. The input data on counter activity can be attendant minutes of employees at counters in the post office and the outputs at the counter can be counter transactions in minutes (i.e., counter operation multiplied by standard time for that operation) for all kinds of mail related activities, after sales service such as enquiries regarding delay in deliveries of registered articles, etc., and financial services. Each of the three outputs would be aggregation of different types of operations made for customers at the counter. The study can also be extended to cover back office operations such as accounting, cash operations, aggregated in minutes. Offices could be classified into small, medium and large offices and data collected from each of these offices. The branch post offices can be a special area of study on cost elasticity. Cost elasticity less than one can have important implications on pricing policies for retail activities through these post offices, as for example, pricing decisions based on variable cost principle, etc.

Econometric analysis of mail volume demand in case of India Post can also be done. Studies based on such analysis in case of the United States found the following variables to be important: real price, real GDP per capita, size of pre-sort discount relative to business labour costs, proxy for number of financial accounts per household, volume of addressed mail. Some other variables which may be significant for the demand function could be the level of activities of telecommunications and insurance in the country. Per capita non-cash financial transactions (thereby implying more bills to be sent to consumers), per capita newspaper consumption, number of retail firms per hundred inhabitants may also be found to be significant as explanatory variables of mail volume. Suitable policy guidelines and future path can then be suggested for India Post.

BIBLIOGRAPHY

Abramovitz, M., (1956): *Resource and Output Trends in the United States since 1870*, National Bureau of Economic Research Occasional Paper 52.

Afriat, S.N., (1972): Efficiency Estimation of Production Functions, *International Economic Review*, Vol. 13, No. 3, pp. 568-598.

Aigner, D. and S. Chu, (1968): On Estimating the Industry Production Function, *American Economic Review*, Vol. 58, pp. 826-839.

Aigner, D.J., C.A.K. Lovell and P. Schmidt, (1977): Formulation and Estimation of Stochastic Frontier Production Function Models, *Journal of Econometrics*, Vol. 6, pp. 21-37.

Awerbuch, S. and A. Preston, (2000): Postal ABC: What are the Reasonable Expectations? in M.A. Crew and P.R. Kleindorfer (eds.) *Current Directions in Postal Reform*, Boston: Kluwer Academic Publishers.

Banker, R.D. and R.C. Morey, (1986): The Use of Categorical Variables in Data Envelopment Analysis, *Management Science, Vol.* 32, No. 12, pp. 1613-1627.

Battese, G.E. and T.J. Coelli, (1995): A Model for Technical Inefficiency Effects in a Stochastic Frontier Production Function for Panel Data, *Empirical Economics,* Vol. 20, pp. 325-332.

Bauer, P.W., (1990a): Decomposing TFP Growth in the Presence of Cost Inefficiency, Non-constant Returns to Scale, and Technological Progress, *Journal of Productivity Analysis,* Vol. 1, No. 4, pp. 287-301.

Bauer, P.W., (1990b): Recent Developments in the Econometric Estimation of Frontiers, *Journal of Econometrics,* Vol. 46, pp. 39-56.

Baumol, W.J. and D.F. Bradford, (1970): Optimal Departures from Marginal Cost Pricing, *American Economic Review*, Vol. 60, pp. 265-283.

Bernard, S., R. Cohen, M. Robinson, B. Roy, J. Toledano, J. Waller, and S. Xenakis, (2002): *Delivery Cost Heterogeneity and Vulnerability to Entry* in M.A. Crew and P.R. Kleindorfer (eds.), *Postal and Delivery Services: Delivering on Competition*, Boston: Kluwer Academic Publishers.

Bjurek, H., (1996): The Malmquist Total Factor Productivity Index, *Scandinavian Journal of Economics*, Vol. 98, pp. 303-313.

Bjurek, H., L. Hjalmarsson, F.R. Forsund, (1990): Deterministic Parametric and Non-Parametric Estimation of Efficiency in Service Production—A Comparison, *Journal of Econometrics,* Vol. 46, pp. 213-227.

Bradley, M.D., and J. Colvin, (2000): *Measuring the Cost of Universal Service for Posts* in M.A. Crew and P.R. Kleindorfer (eds.) Current Directions in Postal Reform, Boston: Kluwer Academic Publishers.

Bradley, M.D., and J. Colvin, (1999): *Productivity and Technical Change in a Public Service Enterprise* in M.A. Crew and P.R. Kleindorfer (eds.) Emerging Competition in Postal and Delivery Services, Boston: Kluwer Academic Publishers.

Bradley, M.D., and J. Colvin, (2001): *The Role of the Monopoly Product in the Cost of Universal Service* in M.A. Crew and P.R. Kleindorfer (eds.) Future Directions in Postal Reform, Boston: Kluwer Academic Publishers.

Bradley, M.D., C.S. Brehm, J. Colvin and W.M. Takis, (1999): *Emprirical Estimation of Incremental Costs for the US Postal Service* in M.A. Crew and P.R. Kleindorfer (eds.) Emerging Competition in Postal and Delivery Services, Boston: Kluwer Academic Publishers.

Bradley, M.D., J. Colvin and J. Panzar, (1997): *Issues in Measuring Incremental Cost in a Multi-function Enterprise* in M.A. Crew and P.R. Kleindorfer (eds.) Managing Change in the Postal and Delivery Industries, Boston: Kluwer Academic Publishers.

Burns, P., I. Carslake and G. Houpis, (2002): *Brand Loyalty and Limited Entry in Postal Market* in M.A. Crew and P.R. Kleindorfer (eds.) Postal and Delivery Services: Delivering on Competition, Boston: Kluwer Academic Publishers.

Caves, D.W., L.R. Christensen, and W.E. Diewert, (1982): The Economic Theory of Index Numbers and the Measurement of Input, Output and Productivity, *Econometrica*, Vol. 50, No. 6.

Cazals, C., P. Duchemin, J.P. Florens, B. Roy and Olivier Vialaneix, (2002): *An Econometric Study of Cost Elasticity in the Activities of Post Office Counter* in M.A. Crew and P.R. Kleindorfer (eds.) Postal and Delivery Services: Pricing, Productivity, Regulation and Strategy, Boston: Kluwer Academic Publishers.

Cazals, C., and J.P. Florens, (2002): *Econometrics of Mail Demand: A Comparison between Cross-section and Dynamic Data* in M.A. Crew and P.R. Kleindorfer (eds.) Postal and Delivery Services: Delivering on Competition, Boston: Kluwer Academic Publishers.

Cazals, C., J.P. Florens and B. Roy, (2001): *An Analysis of Some Specific Cost Drivers in the Delivery Activity* in M.A. Crew and P.R. Kleindorfer (eds.) Future Directions in Postal Reform, Boston: Kluwer Academic Publishers.

Charnes, A., W.W. Cooper and E. Rhodes, (1978): Measuring the Efficiency of Decision-Making Units, *European Journal of Operational Research*, Vol. 2, No. 6, pp. 429-444.

Christensen, L.R., D.W. Jorgenson and L.J. Lau, (1973): Transcendental Logarithmic Production Frontiers, *The Review of Economics and Statistics* 55:1 (February) 28-45.

Coelli, T.J., (1996a): A Guide to DEAP Version 2.1: A Data Envelopment Analysis (Computer) Programme, *CEPA Working Papers 8/96*, Department of Econometrics, University of New England, Armidale, Australia.

Coelli, T.J., (1996b): A Guide to FRONTIER Version 4.1: A Computer Programme for Stochastic Frontier Production and Cost Function Estimation, CEPA *Working Papers 7/96*, Department of Econometrics, University of New England, Armidale Australia.

Coelli, T.J., and S. Perelman, (1996a): Efficiency Measurement, Multiple-output Technologies and Distance Functions: With Application to European Railways, *CREPP 96/05*, University of Liege, Liege.

Coelli, T.J., and S. Perelman, (1996b): A Comparison of Parametric and Non-Parametric Distance Functions: With Application to European Railways, *CREPP Working Paper 96/11*, University of Liege, Liege.

Coelli, T.J. and S. Perelman, (1999): A Comparison of Parametric and Non-parametric Distance Functions: With Application to European Railways, *European Journal of Operational Research* 117, 326-339.

Coelli, T.J., and S. Perelman, (2000): Technical Efficiency of European Railways: A Distance Function Approach, *Applied Economics*, 32, 1967-1976.

Coelli, T.J., D.S. Prasad Rao, and G.E. Battese, (1998): *An Introduction to Efficiency and Productivity Analysis*, Boston: Kluwer Academic Publishers.

Cornwell C., P. Schmidt, and R.C. Sickles, (1990): Production Frontiers with Cross-Sectional and Time-Series Variation in Efficiency Levels, *Journal of Econometrics* 46, 185-200.

Cowing, T.G. and R.E. Stevenson, (1981): *Introduction: Productivity Measurement and Regulated Industries,* in T.G. Cowing and R.E. Stevenson (eds.), Productivity Measurement in Regulated Industries, Academic Press, 03-14.

Cremer H, A. Grimaud and J. Laffont, (2000): *The Cost of Universal Service in the Postal Sector* in Michael A. Crew and Paul R. Kleindorfer (eds.) Current Directions in Postal Reform, Boston: Kluwer Academic Publishers.

Crew, M.A. and P.R. Kleindorfer, (2000): *Cost Estimation and Economically Efficient Pric,* in Michael A. Crew and Paul R. Kleindorfer (eds.) Current Directions in Postal Reform, Boston: Kluwer Academic Publishers.

Crew, M.A. and P.R. Kleindorfer, (2000): *Liberalization and the Universal Service Obligation in Postal Service* in Michael A. Crew and Paul R. Kleindorfer (eds.), Current Directions in Postal Reform, Boston: Kluwer Academic Publishers.

Crew, M.A. and P.R. Kleindorfer, (2002): *Balancing Access and the Universal Service Obligation* in Michael A. Crew and Paul R. Kleindorfer (eds.) Postal and Delivery Services: Delivering on Competition, Boston: Kluwer Academic Publishers.

Denny, M., M. Fuss, and L. Waverman, (1981): *The Measurement and Interpretation of Total Factor Productivity in Regulated Industries, with an Application to Canadian Telecommunications* in T.G. Cowing and R.E. Stevenson (eds.) Productivity Measurement in Regulated Industries, Academic Press, 179-218.

Deprins, D., L. Simar and H. Tulkens, (1984): *Measuring Labour-Efficiency in Post Offices* in M. Marchand, P. Pestieau and H. Tulkens (eds.) The Performance of Public Enterprises: Concepts and Measurement, Amsterdam: North-Holland.

Diewert, E.W., (1981): *The Theory of Total Factor Productivity Measurement in Regulated Industries* in T.G. Cowing and R.E. Stevenson (eds.) Productivity Measurement in Regulated Industries, Academic Press, 17-44.

Donder, P.D., H. Cremer, J. Florens, A. Grimaud and F. Rodriguez, (2001): *Uniform Pricing and Postal Market Liberalization* in Michael A. Crew and Paul R. Kleindorfer (eds.), Future Directions in Postal Reform, Boston: Kluwer Academic Publishers.

Fare, R., and S. Grosskopf, (1992): Malmquist Productivity Indexes and Fisher Ideal Indexes, *Economic Journal* 102(4) 158-160.

Fare, R., and D. Primont, (1995): *Multi-Output Production and Duality: Theory and Applications*, Boston: Kluwer Academic Publishers.

Fare, R., S. Grosskopf, and C.A.K. Lovell, (1994): *Production Frontiers*, Cambridge University Press, Cambridge.

Fare, R., S. Grosskopf, M. Norris and Z. Zhang, (1994): Productivity Growth, Technical Progress, and Efficiency Change in Industrialized Countries, *American Economic Review*, 84, 66-83.

Fare, R., S. Grosskopf, S. Yaisawarng, S.K. Li and Z. Wang, (1990): Productivity Growth in Illinois Electric Utilities, *Resources and Energy* 12: 383-398.

Farrell, M.J., (1957): The Measurement of Productive Efficiency, *Journal of the Royal Statistical Society*, Series A, (General) Part III, Vol. 120, pp. 253-290.

Faulhaber G.R., (1975): Cross Subsidization: Pricing in Public Enterprises, *The American Economic Review*, Vol. 65, No. 5, 966-977.

Forsund, F.R. and L. Hjalmarsson, (1979): Frontier Production Functions and Technical Progress: A Study of General Milk Production in Swedish Dairy Plants, *Economic Journal*, 89: 294-315.

Forsund, F.R., C.A.K. Lovell and P. Schmidt, (1980): A Survey of Frontier Production Functions and of their Relationship to Efficiency Measurement, *Journal of Econometrics* 13, 5-25.

Fried, H.O., C.A.K. Lovell and S.S. Schmidt, (1993): *The Measurement of Productive Efficiency: Techniques and Applications,* Oxford University Press, New York.

Fuentes, H.J., E. Grifell-Tatje, S. Perelman, (2001): A Parametric Distance Function Approach for Malmquist Productivity Index Estimation, *Journal of Productivity Analysis*, 15, 79-94

Gazzei, D.S., C. Pace and G. Scarfiglieri, (2002): *On the Output Elasticity of the Activities of Post Office Counters in Italy* in Michael A. Crew and Paul R. Kleindorfer (eds.) Postal and Delivery Services: Delivering on Competition, Boston: Kluwer Academic Publishers.

Gollop, F.M. and M.J. Roberts, (1981): The Sources of Economic Growth in the US Electric Power Industry in T.G. Cowing and R.E. Stevenson (eds.) Productivity Measurement in Regulated Industries, Academic Press, 107-143.

Government of India, Demands for Grants of Department of Posts, (1996-97, 1997-98, 1998-99, 1999-2000, 2000-01, 2001-02, 2002-03, 2003-04, 2004-05, 2005-06, 2006-07, 2007-08).

Government of India, Department of Posts, Annual Report, (1996-97, 1997-98, 1998-99, 1999-2000, 2000-01, 2001-02, 2002-03, 2003-04, 2004-05, 2005-06, 2006-07, 2007-08).

Government of India, Department of Posts, Book of Information, (1996-97, 1997-98, 1998-99, 1999-2000, 2000-01, 2001-02, 2002-03, 2003-04, 2004-05, 2005-06).

Government of India, Department of Posts, Expert Committee on Excellence in Postal Services, December 1988.

Government of India, Planning Commission, Report of the Working Group on Posts, Tenth Five Year Plan (2002-07), September 2001.

Government of India, The Indian Telegraph (Amendment) Act, 2003.

Greene, W.H., (1980a): Maximum Likelihood Estimation of Econometric Frontier Functions, *Journal of Econometrics* 13, 27-56.

Greene, W.H., (1980b): On the Estimation of a Flexible Frontier Production Model, *Journal of Econometrics* 13, 101-115.

Greene, W.H., (1990): A Gamma-distributed Stochastic Frontier Model. *Journal of Econometrics* 46, 141-163.

Greene, W.H., (1993): *The Econometric Approach to Efficiency Analysis* in Fried, H.O., C.A.K. Lovell and S.S. Schmidt (eds.) The Measurement of Productive Efficiency: Techniques and Applications, Oxford University Press, 68-119.

Greene, W.H., (1997): *Frontier Production Functions* in M.H. Pesaran and P. Schmidt (eds.) Handbook of Applied Econometrics, Volume II: Microeconomics, Oxford: Blackwell Publishers Ltd.

Greene, W.H., (2003): *Econometric Analysis*, 5th Edition, Pearson Education.

Grifell-Tatje, E. and C.A.K. Lovell, (1995): A Note on the Malmquist Productivity Index, *Economics Letters*, 47, 169-175

Grosskopf, S., (1993): *Efficiency and Productivity* in Fried, H.O., C.A.K. Lovell and S.S. Schmidt (eds.) The Measurement of Productive Efficiency: Techniques and Applications, Oxford University Press, 160-194.

Hulten, C.R., (1973): Divisia Index Numbers, *Econometrica*, Vol. 41, No. 6, 1017-1025.

Jha, R., M.N. Murty and B. Sahni, (1992): Technical Efficiency in the Public Sector: An Analysis of the State Electricity Boards in India, *Indian Economic Review*, Special Number, 385-395.

Jha, R., M.N. Murty and S. Paul, (1990): *Pricing of Postal Services in India*, National Institute of Public Finance and Policy, Delhi.

Johnston, J. and J. DiNardo, (1997): *Econometric Methods,* New York: McGraw-Hill.

Jondrow, J., C.A.K. Lovell, I.S. Materov and P. Schmidt, (1982): On the Estimation of Technical Inefficiency in the Stochastic Frontier Production Function Model, *Journal of Econometrics* 19, 233-238.

Kopp, R.J., and W.E. Diewert, (1982): The Decomposition of Frontier Cost Function Deviations into Measures of Technical and Allocative Efficiency, *Journal of Econometrics* 19, 319-331.

Kumbhakar, S.C., (1990): Production Frontiers, Panel Data and Time Varying Technical Inefficiency. *Journal of Econometrics*, 46, 201-211.

Kumbhakar, S.C. and C.A. Knox Lovell, (2000): *Stochastic Frontier Analysis*, Cambridge University Press.

Laffont, J. and J. Tirole, (1996): Creating Competition Through Interconnection: Theory and Practice, *Journal of Regulatory Economics* 10:227-256.

Lovell, C.A.K., (1993): *Production Frontiers and Productive Efficiency* in Fried, H.O., C.A.K. Lovell and S.S. Schmidt (eds.) The Measurement of Productive Efficiency; Techniques and Applications, Oxford University Press, 3-67.

Lovell, C.A.K., and P. Schmidt, (1988): *A Comparison of Alternative Approaches to the Measurement of Productive Efficiency* in A. Dogramaci and R. Fare (eds.) Studies in Productivity Analysis. Application of Modern Production Theory. Efficiency and Productivity, Boston: Kluwer Academic Publishers.

Maruyama, S. and T. Nakajima, (2002): *The Productivity Analysis of Postal Services: A Global Comparison of Technical Efficiency and Total Factor Productivity* in M.A. Crew and Paul R. Kleindorfer (eds.) Postal and Delivery Services: Delivering on Competition, Kluwer Academic Publishers.

Meeusen, W. and J. Van den Broeck, (1977): Efficiency Estimation from Cobb-Douglas Production Functions with Composed Error, *International Economic Review* 18, 435-444.

Mitchell, R.W., (1999): *Postal Worksharing: Welfare, Technical Efficiency, and Pareto Optimality* in M.A. Crew and Paul R. Kleindorfer (eds.) Emerging Competition in Postal and Delivery Services, Boston: Kluwer Academic Publishers.

Nadiri, M.I. and M.A. Schankerman, (1981): *The Structure of Production, Technological Change, and the Rate of Growth of Total Factor Productivity in the U.S. Bell System* in T.G. Cowing and R.E. Stevenson (eds.) Productivity Measurement in Regulated Industries, Academic Press, 219-247.

Nankervis, J., I. Carslake and Frank Rodriguez, (1999): *How Important Have Price and Quality of Service Been to Mail Volume Growth* in M.A. Crew and Paul R. Kleindorfer (eds.) *Emerging* Competition in Postal and Delivery Services, Boston: Kluwer Academic Publisher.

Nikali, H., (2002): *Productivity and the Substitution between Labour and Capital in Postal Organizations* in M.A. Crew and Paul R. Kleindorfer (eds.) Postal and Delivery Services: Pricing, Productivity, Regulation and Strategy, Boston: Kluwer Academic Publishers.

Nishimizu, M. and J.M. Page Jr., (1982): Total Factor Productivity Growth, Technological Progress and Technical Efficiency Change: Dimensions of Productivity Change in Yugoslavia, 1965-78, *Economic Journal* 92(368) (December): 920-36.

Norswarthy, J.R., S. Jang and W. Shi, (1991): *Productivity and Cost Measurement for the United States Postal Service: Variation among Regions* in M.A. Crew and Paul R. Kleindorfer (eds.) Competition and Innovation in Postal Services Boston: Kluwer Academic Publishers.

Panzar J.C., (2002): *Reconciling Competition, Downstream Access, and Universal Service in Postal Markets* in M.A. Crew and Paul R. Kleindorfer (eds.) Postal and Delivery Services: Delivering on Competition, Boston: Kluwer Academic Publishers.

Perelman, S., and P. Pestieau, (1988): Technical Performance in Public Enterprise: A Comparative Study of Railways and Postal Services, *European Economic Review* 32: 432-441.

Perelman, S. and P. Pestieau, (1994): A Comparative Performance Study of Postal Service: A Productive Efficiency Approach, *Annales d' Economies et de Statistique*.

Pickett, J.T., D.E. Treworgy and A.W.B. Conrad, (2000): *Access Pricing in the Postal Sector: Complexities and Practicalities of the United States Experience* in M.A. Crew and P. R. Kleindorfer (eds.) Current Directions in Postal Reform, Boston: Kluwer Academic Publishers.

Pimenta, A.A., R.G. Santos and S.C. Lagoa, (2000): *Technical Efficiency in CTT-Correios de Portugal* in M.A. Crew and Paul R. Kleindorfer (eds.), Current Directions in Postal Reform, Boston: Kluwer Academic Publishers.

Rodriguez, F., S. Smith and David Storer, (1999): *Estimating the Cost of the Universal Service Obligation in Postal Service* in M.A. Crew and Paul R. Kleindorfer (eds.) Emerging Competition in Postal and Delivery Services, Boston Kluwer Academic Publishers.

Roy, B., (1999): *Technico-Economic Analysis of the Costs of Outside Work in Postal Delivery* in M.A. Crew and Paul R. Kleindorfer (eds.) Emerging Competition in Postal and Delivery Services, Boston: Kluwer Academic Publishers.

Santos, R.G. and S.C. Lagoa, (2001): *The Demand for Direct Mail in Portugal* in M.A. Crew and Paul R. Kleindorfer (eds.) Future Directions in Postal Reform, Boston: Kluwer Academic Publishers.

Scarfiglieri, G. and V.V. Comandini, (2001): *Postal Profits Arise Where People Are* in M.A. Crew and Paul R. Kleindorfer (eds.) Future Directions in Postal Reform, Boston: Kluwer Academic Publishers.

Schmidt, P., (1985-1986): Frontier Production Functions, *Econometric Reviews* 4(2), 289-328.

Schmidt, P. and C.A.K. Lovell, (1979): Estimating Technical and Allocative Inefficiency Relative to Stochastic Production and Cost Functions, *Journal of Econometrics* 9, 343-366.

Schmidt, P., and C.A.K. Lovell, (1980): Estimating Stochastic Production and Cost Frontiers When Technical and Allocative Inefficiency are Correlated, *Journal of Econometrics* 13, 83-100.

Scott, F.A. Jr., (1986): Assessing USA Postal Ratemaking: An Application of Ramsey Prices, *The Journal of Industrial Economics* Vol. XXXIV, 279-290.

Shephard, R.W., (1953): *Cost and Production Functions*, Princeton University Press, Princeton.

Shephard, R.W., (1970): *The Theory of Cost and Production Functions*, Princeton University Press, Princeton.

Soares, J., J. Confraria and A. Pimenta, (2002): *Postal Services Cost Modeling* in M.A. Crew and Paul R. Kleindorfer (eds.) Postal and Delivery Services: Pricing, Productivity, Regulation and Strategy, Boston: Kluwer Academic Publishers.

Solow, R.M., (1957): Technical Change and the Aggregate Production Function, *The Review of Economics and Statistics*, 39: 3, 312-320.

Stevenson, R.E., (1980): Likelihood Functions for Generalized Stochastic Frontier Estimation, *Journal of Econometrics* 13, 57-66.

Subrahmanyam, G., (1993): Productivity Growth in India's Public Sector Banks: 1970-89, *Journal of Quantitative Economics*, Vol. 9, No. 2, 209-223.

Treworgy, D.E., T.M. Sharkey, D.R. Fronk and M.J. Kehoe, (1999): *Price-Cap Regulation in the Postal Sector: An International Comparison and Assessment*, in M.A. Crew and Paul R. Kleindorfer (eds.) Emerging Competition in Postal and Delivery Services, Boston: Kluwer Academic Publishers.

Waterman, R., D. Rubin, N. Thomas and A. Gelman, (2000): *Simulation Modeling for Cost Estimation* in M.A. Crew and Paul R. Kleindorfer (eds.) Current Directions in Postal Reform, Boston: Kluwer Academic Publishers.

Index